THE
INSPIRATIONAL
PARENT

The *Magical* Ingredients for
Effective Parenting

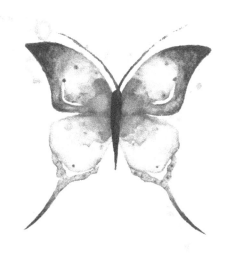

ALEX URBINA

Published by: Be the Change Publishing
Santa Clarita, California
Copyright @ Alex Urbina Life Coaching 1998 - 2017

The Inspirational Parent and The Magical Ingredients for Effective Parenting is a trademark of Alex Urbina. All Rights Reserved.
www.theinspirationalparent.com
www.alexurbina.com

Publisher's Cataloging-In-Publication Data
(Prepared by The Donohue Group, Inc.)
Names: Urbina, Alex.
Title: The inspirational parent: the magical ingredients for effective parenting / Alex Urbina.
Description: Santa Clarita, California: Be the Change Publishing, [2017] | Series: The magical ingredients for effective parenting; v. 1 | Includes bibliographical references.
Identifiers: LCCN 2017906917 | ISBN 978-0-9989343-0-3 (print) | ISBN 0-9989343-0-5 (print)
Subjects: LCSH: Parenting. | Parent and child.
Classification: LCC HQ755.85.U73 2017 (print) | LCC HQ755.85 (eBook) | DDC 306.874–dc23

ISBN-13: 978-0998934303
ISBN-10: 0998934305
Library of Congress Control Number 2017906917

Please Note: All information presented in this book is for informational purposes only. It is not specific medical advice for any individual and should not be construed as medical consultation or instruction. No action should be taken solely on the basis of this book's contents. Readers are advised to consult a health professional about any issue regarding their health and well-being, or the health and well-being of your child. The author and publisher specifically disclaim any liability that is incurred from the use or application of the contents of this book.

Disclaimer:

This publication is sold with the understanding that the author is not engaged in rendering psychological, medical, or other professional services. If expert assistance or counseling is needed, the services of a competent professional should be sought.

For ordering information or special discounts for bulk purchases, please email themagicalingredients@gmail.com

Printed in the United States of America.

DEDICATION

I dedicate this book to my Father and Mother Alexander V. Urbina and Gloria A. Urbina. Thank you, both for loving me unconditionally, and for loving me with every ounce of love you have within you.

CONTENTS

FORWARD

Our children enter our lives so that we can awaken to our higher selves. They are, unequivocally, the clearest mirrors to our greatest potential. It is through our relationship with them that we can access who we once were and could have been.

They not only show us how to live in the present moment in a way few others can but also remind us of how this lack of present-moment living has skewed our relationship to ourselves and others. When we dare to look in the mirror they provide to us, we begin to remember how we left pieces of our authentic self back in our childhood and try to discover ways to re-integrate them back into our lives.

In this powerful ode to the power of the parenting process, Alex shows us how to commit to our children's growth and transformation. He reminds us that we do indeed possess the skills and ways of being that can best increase our children's resilience: we have just forgotten how to access them.

Alex writes in a way that evokes courage to create the changes we need to make to help our children thrive, no matter what the challenge, even if we have to fully let go of our present-day iterations and re-invent ourselves to allow for our children to enter freedom, love and grace.

Written with deep reflection and insight, this wonderful book allows us to remember the depth of our influence in our children's lives and that they came to us to show us how we can grow into our fullest selves. Stepping away from fear and control, Alex speaks to the power of conscious parenting and the ways in which it can irrevocably transform not only the parent and the child, but the entire planet.

I always say that the parental evolution is the solution to healing the planet. It is books like these that give us the tools to awaken out of slumber so that we can be of best service to ourselves, our families and our children.

Dr. Shefali Tsabary
NYT bestselling author of The Awakened Family
Clinical Psychologist and International Speaker

ACKNOWLEDGMENTS

I would like to sincerely express my gratitude to all of the people that have supported my commitment to complete this book. To all those who have participated in focus groups, read, wrote, gave feedback, allowed me to interview you, to share your contributions, assisted in the editing, proofreading, and design; I thank you.

I would like to thank Be the Change Publishing for seeing the vision and publishing this book. Above all, I want to thank my amazing, and dear wife Yvette Urbina, for your unwavering support; as well as my three incredible kids Mark, Jazmine, and Sasha for supporting me. You have always been willing to share, and sacrifice your time with me for a higher purpose; I will never forget that.

I would like to thank Shira Bush "The Book Creator" for your relentless commitment to my success, and your guidance, and leadership. I would like to thank Celia Taghdiri, and Kirsten Quinn, for all of your late nights of editing, for professionalism, and excellence. I want to thank Circe Denyer for your talented editing, and formatting experience, and being my last stand for greatness.

I would like to thank Jazmine Urbina, and Jeri Seratti-Goldman for your creative passion, and valuable input. I would like to thank Shannon Gonzalez for your beautiful and creative artwork, illustrations, and book cover design.

I would like to thank Patti Handy for your author advice, and Carl Goldman, Jeri Seratti-Goldman for your loyal and steadfast support, and guidance.

I would like to honor and give my biggest heartfelt gratitude to all of the contributing authors to this book, who are unselfishly sharing your wisdom, insight, and love with all of our readers. Each one of you has impacted my life in a profound way. I am in awe of you, and the lightwork you share with the world: Dr. Ray Blanchard, Bettie J. Spruill, Charlene Afremow, Raphael Natale, Gabriel Nossovitch, Sue Keith, Terilynn Werner, Patricia Villamil, Joe & Wendy Amara, Kelly Sanchez, and Roxy Hernandez.

INTRODUCTION

I received a call one day from a frantic mother; her voice was soft yet severe. I could tell she had been crying, she sounded crushed and defeated. It was the mother of a sixteen-year-old boy whom I knew very well; his name was Daniel.

Daniel was a very bright boy, highly intuitive, creative and talented in many ways. He had all the right tools to become someone of great importance to the world; to make a huge contribution in more ways than one.

After I had realized who I was talking to, I greeted Daniel's mom with a very compassionate "Hello."

The next thing I heard, was Daniel's mom say to me "I've lost control Alex! Daniel does not listen to me anymore, and he doesn't respect me either."

After a very intense hour and a half conversation with Daniel's mother, I was finally able to get her to see that she never really had control of her son at all.

It was all an illusion! - and I was also able to get her to see that this new moment of clarity was going to be one of her greatest moments as a parent; the moment to start a new journey of conscious parenting.

I have been coaching Daniel's mother for the last year and a half; she has been one of the many inspirational parents whom I have been honored to know.

She is not perfect, no parent is.

What makes her so inspirational is her willingness to be wrong about how she was parenting her son, courageously open minded, and rigorously committed to learning how to reinvent herself.

She would eventually become the mom that Daniel needed from her; to be heard, to be validated, to be encouraged to follow his own passions and discover his own purpose driven life.

One of the biggest parenting frustrations happens when parents learn they no longer have control over their children - being discouraged that they no longer listen to you, take your advice, or can see that all you want is the best for them.

At some point in the adolescent journey, young people discover they can think for themselves, make their own decisions independently, and utilize their voice.

At this pivotal moment, the average parent may experience difficulties adjusting to their child's newly discovered independence, so it's best to be prepared!

One of the secrets to extraordinary parenting is realizing that the "controlling style" parenting model historically applied may not be as effective in the 21st Century.

If you want to make a huge impact on your children, inspiring and empowering them to be the self-directed leaders you envision them to be, this book is for you.

When most parents realize they need help, they often seek advice from a friend, counselor, a therapist or a spiritual leader.

Although some professionals may be able to help, I firmly believe you already have everything it takes to create an extraordinary relationship with your children, fostering love, trust, and a cohesive partnership.

I want to help you discover this before that time comes – or now if it is occurring – or after years of conflict and disappointment.

For over 20 years, I have been working with both teens and parents all over the world, helping them discover their full potential, reclaiming their love, commitment, and dedication to each other.

In this book, I share with you some of my own parenting insight, while learning from my mistakes raising my three children, as well as the insight I have learned from thousands of teenagers in training rooms all around the world.

I have reached out on your behalf and asked a handful of incredibly wise, compassionate, and selfless leaders in the field of Transformational Training and Personal Development, to contribute their insight for you and your parenting growth.

If you desire, this book will inspire you to reach your next level of parenting.

In order to help your children develop into loving, powerful, confident and responsible leaders, you must adapt a new style of parenting; the "coaching style."

Our coaching style parenting model will help you become the inspiring and empowering parent/mentor your children need. This model also guides children to be mentally, emotionally and spiritually centered to thrive in today's world.
It requires you to learn, discover and grow interpersonally, reinventing yourself to create deep and meaningful relationships.

This book will guide you along your journey of conscious parenting, help you reach a more advanced level that mentors and coaches need to empower others.

Throughout this book, you will discover and learn more about the Magical Ingredients for Effective Parenting as they were taught to me.

Most people first learn how to "do" something to produce a result, but very few learn how to first "BE" something.

What you are not going to learn in this book is what you need to "do" as a parent to create successful results. Instead, you will learn who it is you need to "BE."

In each chapter of the book, we will review a new distinction to help you better understand how to master that way of being, while becoming a more conscious parent, proud of the legacy you will leave behind for your own children to pass on to your grandchildren.

THE
INSPIRATIONAL
PARENT

DISTINCTION ONE
BE – DO – HAVE

A self-discovery opportunity in the summer of 2012 forever changed my life. My 6-year-old daughter consistently lied to me whenever I asked her questions about things that occurred in our home.

After several months of her continuous dishonesty and my frustration, finally, I took a moment to deeply reflect on who I was in her presence that allowed her to repeatedly lie to my face.

Through my own relentless and honest self-reflection, it dawned on me that whenever she would lie to me, I projected my own fear, anger, disappointment, and frustration onto her.

With this newfound awareness, I was able to recognize and identify that who I was being in that moment as a father was a direct reflection of what I was actually doing as a father.

Being fearful, angry, disappointed and frustrated produced these different scenarios, during which I could see what I was actually doing as a parent:

- Talking to her in a frustrated tone

- Making her feel bad for lying to me

- Making facial expressions that manifested my disappointment

- Looking down at her with disgrace

- Badgering her until she gave me an answer I wanted to hear

- Looking for something in her to try to fix

- Reprimanding her and taking things away from her

- Repeatedly pointing out how bad it is to lie, harping on the problem

- Using body language that expressed my distrust, doubt, and disbelief

It appeared to me from my daughter's point of view; I was repeatedly confrontational and aggressive with her whenever she lied. My behavior was producing the same result from her – more lies. What I had realized was that I was part of the problem not part of the solution.

As I sat there in silence wondering what to do next, I remembered the Be-Do-Have model I had been taught years earlier.

Be-Do-Have is a universal principle that helps you focus more on who you are *"being"* in each life situation rather than what it is you think you need to *"do."* It helps you create extraordinary results that otherwise may not be possible.

At that moment, I made a conscious decision to change my behavior with my daughter. I made an agreement with myself that the next time I caught her being dishonest, I would choose to *be* with her in a new and empowering way.

I began to *be* with her in a more loving, vulnerable, understanding and compassionate way.

One afternoon I walked into my kids' bedroom and noticed a drawing on the wall, freshly painted with crayon. I wasn't angry upon noticing the drawing. I just wanted to know who had done it, so I can teach them not to do it again and show them how to clean it up.

I gathered my three kids and asked them, "Who drew this picture on the wall?"

All I got was silence for about 10 seconds, and then each one of them said: "Not me, Dad," followed by my oldest son and youngest daughter immediately looking at my 6-year-old.

(Kids are so funny they have no idea they give themselves away.)

At this moment, I remembered the agreement I made with myself, to *be* more loving, vulnerable, and compassionate.

I went into my heart and imagined what it might feel like to be so afraid of getting in trouble by your dad, facing the possibility of being yelled at or punished.

To my surprise, shifting who I was *being* with her caused me to *do* my parenting in a new and powerful way. The new choices I was making, while interacting with my little girl, were unique, refreshing, and unorthodox. It took an enormous amount of courage and trust on my part, but it was well worth it.

For a brief moment, I witnessed the contrast between what I was doing versus who I was being while we were together.

Being more loving, vulnerable, understanding, and compassionate with her created new behavior patterns for me as a parent.

These are the behavior changes I noticed:

- My tone was softer; my voice reflected forgiveness
- I asked her open-ended questions, such as, Now what? How can we fix this?

- I sat down on the floor to make myself appear smaller than her

- I sat her on my lap and held her hand as we talked

- My voice cracked, and I cried as I told her I trust her with all my heart

- We cried together, and she apologized to me

- I shared with her that I too don't always tell the truth

- I gave her new options

- I reminded her how amazing she is

- I reassured her that her family trusted her and loved her

- I made an agreement with her that if she tells me the truth about something she did wrong, I will not get angry

It was a profound moment. I was inspired by her level of maturity. I was in awe of her capacity to interact with me the way she did. I was proud of her and proud of myself for being willing to shift and create a new approach, in essence, creating a new way of being.

This experience changed me forever. It opened my heart and my eyes to see I was capable of creating new results with my children.

This was a pivotal moment for my daughter, resulting in an ethical course correction that would later be the framework for living a life of integrity and revere. It was a new behavior pattern for her to embrace and practice.

For me, it was a huge eye-opener, a profound breakthrough. I remember saying to myself, "If only I could continue to get out of my own way, start taking responsibility for the results of my relationships and continue to discover who my kids need me to be, so they could discover and develop their own greatness. Then, I will have fulfilled my duty as a father, with honor and dignity.

The Be-Do-Have model is a universal principle and a very powerful and creative process. When applied correctly, it will custom design our lives and alter the results in our favor.

When you truly understand how it works, and use it in your life, the application of Be-Do-Have can and will support you in becoming a more empowering and influential parent.

I shared with you what I have learned and continue to learn from my personal journey of practicing and living by the Be-Do-Have model. Later, I will share how it's changing my life by helping me discover the true power I've always had within me.

I'm learning there is a distinct difference between *being* and *doing.* That kind of understanding and clarity has emphatically and positively affected my relationships with my kids and my effectiveness as a father, and my ability to lead my family.

Looking back at my childhood, I realize now I was only taught how to *do* specific things in my life to get results – not be in it in a way that would profoundly alter the results – in ways I could not ever imagine. During my adolescence, I was taught that to *have* the results I wanted in my life; I had to "work for it or earn it."

I had to do more, do better, do differently, to achieve, accomplish, and have the desired results.

Society also seems to have played a part in promoting and affirming action-oriented results based on the "Doing-ness."

I don't want you to hear that the *doing* is not important because it is. *Doing* is an absolute necessity when it comes to accomplishing our goals. However, I want to emphasize it's not the only component.

Focusing more on who I am *being,* while I am *doing* what it is I need to do to accomplish the aspired results, has been more productive for me in my relationships with my children, my wife, my business associates, and everyone else with whom I engage.

Throughout my journey, I've discovered, when it comes to relationship goals, *being-ness* is the true foundation to build successful relationships.

In the course of creating and manifesting results in my life, the *doing* is secondary in nature. The primary component is my inner quality. It's who I am *being* and how I am expressing myself to others that make the biggest difference and ultimate impact.

Think about it. If *doing* was the main ingredient when it came to creating successful relationships, someone would have already created the perfect to-do list, packaged it and sold it as the perfect blueprint for successful relationships.

I'm not saying that what you *do* in your relationships is not important. What I am saying is that who you are *being* in your relationships is the magical ingredient that opens many more possibilities that you may not have otherwise been able to access.

The magical ingredient I refer to is the essence of who you really are, what you are really made of, who you choose to *be* in your life; the authentic you.

At a certain point in my journey as a young man and father, I discovered this to be true: There is a mighty spirit within me. It is a powerful life force, an energy, a light, a loving being, equipped with feelings, emotions, and experiences uniquely designed with the ability for self-expression while assisting me to produce the desired results in my relationships.

I learned through my own self-awareness that I have the ability to access different ways of *being* within myself to produce different results in my relationships.

After learning all the different ways of *being*, I compiled a list of the ones that are important to me and imperative for my growth – ones that enhance my ability to relate to myself and others.

I told myself, "If I could master these ways of *being*, I would surely become the kind of father I could be proud of; the kind of parent my kids would feel safe opening up to and be inspired by."

Here is my list identifying the different ways of being. Here are the qualities that have helped me become a better father, husband, son, brother, uncle, coach, friend, and more importantly a better leader.

Ways of *Being*

Loving	Compassionate	Vulnerable	Present
Authentic	Understanding	Patient	Forgiving
Connected	Expressive	Inviting	Open
Grateful	Affectionate	Tolerant	Secure
Playful	Committed	Responsible	Trusting

I invite you to take a moment to evaluate yourself using this list. Reflect on your current relationship with your child(ren) and score yourself on a scale of 0-100% in how well you think you're mastering each way of *being* in your relationships; 100% is the highest score.

When most parents evaluate themselves in my Life Coaching practice, they seem to automatically see themselves *being* all of these, all of the time; therefore, they give themselves high scores. It's what I call, "The Great Illusion."

Many parents know themselves to be all of these great qualities, and as much as I honor parents, I would never doubt their sincere intentions. I want to present a possibility that the way parents think we are being experienced by our own kids, may not accurately reflect how our kids experience us.

When working with parents who seem to be 100% honest and authentic in their evaluations, most of their lists look like this:

Ways of Being Evaluation List

Loving	Compassionate	Vulnerable	Authentic
90%	75%	10%	60%
Present	Patient	Understanding	Forgiving
40%	60%	75%	65%
Connected	Open	Inviting	Expressive
60%	70%	30%	75%
Affectionate	Tolerant	Grateful	Secure
75%	70%	75%	60%

Responsible	Committed	Playful	Trusting
80%	50%	40%	70% .

Bear in mind; this evaluation list doesn't take into consideration that our loved ones don't necessarily experience us the same way we perceive ourselves.

When someone other than a parent – i.e. life coach, therapist, psychologist, aunt, uncle, grandparent – asks a child to rate his or her parent, most kids give scores about 20% lower than the scores parents give themselves. For example, if you scored yourself at 90% in the loving category, it's likely your kids would rate you at 70%. What I have found to be a more accurate reflection is somewhere in the middle, like 80%.

When I finally got real with my own personal evaluation, I saw the gaps between my honest self-assessment and where I thought my full potential could take me, as the father I aspired to *be*.

"The Gap" represents the work I still need to complete within myself, the areas of improvement.

Every time one of my kids would act out or talk back to me, I would ask myself: "Who am I *being* or who am I not *being* to make them think it's ok to be so disrespectful to me?"

I immediately thought about the gap. What's still in the gap for me to work on? Obviously, there is a higher level of *being-ness* for me to access, for them to respect me ALL the time. My ego doesn't want me to acknowledge that there is more required of me.

Then my spirit would say to me, "Alex, if only you could have been more present, vulnerable, understanding, and more compassionate for them, just maybe they wouldn't have dumped all of their frustrations on you. Maybe they would have felt as if they were being heard, that you were listening to them, that what they were feeling was validated, that they were respected by you, and in return, they would have shown you all the respect and appreciation you expect from them."

Through years of practicing to master the different ways of *being,* in rigorous pursuit to be the best possible father, I've realized that who I am *being* as a father is way more relevant than what I *do* as a father.

"People don't care how much you know until they know how much you care."- Theodore Roosevelt

This quote reminds me that before I can empower, influence, and inspire my kids in their lives, I must first connect with their hearts; they must first know I absolutely love them, care for them and have their best interest at hand.

Words are not enough.

It reminds me I can have the best advice, the best coaching or best guidance for them; yet none of it can land if I can't help them be more open with me.

Quite often, we parents think words are enough or that they should be sufficient. In part, we feel we have more wisdom than our children, and because of that, they should listen to us.

Today's youth, don't really care how wise their parents are. They just need to know that they matter to us, that we deeply care about them, and that they can trust us. They yearn for an authentic and meaningful connection with us; a one-of-a-kind bond that unites us.

Sometimes the *doing-ness* in our parenting looks like we:

- Give unsolicited advice
- Identify what they did wrong
- Ground them
- Yell
- Project our fears and disappointments onto them
- Don't make eye contact when they try to share
- Talk over them when they need to be heard and validated

- Repeatedly remind them what they did wrong, or keep doing wrong.

- Do things for them instead of empowering them to act independently

From my experience as a father and teen trainer, I know those tactics and ways are far less effective for today's youth.

In my journey of conscious parenting, I am learning my kids first need me to *be* the dad they require from me. Then once I'm being the dad they need – connected, trustworthy, and compassionate, I can now *do* what a dad does – From this place I now can *have* an extraordinary relationship with my kids; one where I can empower, inspire and influence them.

Today's youth need to connect, feel and experience you. If you have not yet learned to express yourself the way your child would like, then that may *be* the reason why you are experiencing resistance and pushback from them.

Most of the behavioral issues we experience from our kids are symptoms of an underlying issue called, "Mom & Dad, I need something more specific from you, and I don't know how to ask for it yet."

You're probably wondering how I would know this? I've heard the cries of teenagers all over the world, from training room to training room for over 20 years. It's always the same.

What they want and need from you most is to look at the Ways of Being list and master being those abilities then summon the courage to implement them in your relationships.

Be and *do* that for them, and watch your relationships blossom, as your kids transform right before your eyes.

I will explain the *Be-Do-Have* model in more detail. To do this effectively, I have to first explain two other models.

Most of us human beings have forgotten that we are "*beings.*" I say forgot because when we were babies, we knew. As we grew up in a society that fosters competition, we slowly learned how to *do* our life, not *be* in our life.

The more we *do,* the better we get at it, and the better we get at it, the more we forget about *being.*

As you get good at *doing*, you adopt the *Do-Have-Be* model of life.

If I *do* this or that, and *do* more of it, *doing* it better and differently, I will have the things I want, more money, a better car, a new career, a different relationship; and as soon as I have all of those things, I will finally "BE" happy, free, noticed, important, and loved, etc.

Do-Have-Be

One of the drawbacks to this model is that it's co-dependent. What you have is dependent on what you *do* and who you're *being* is dependent on what you *have.*

In order to keep *being* happy, you need to keep *having* money, and in order to keep *having* money, you have to keep doing what you do.

This *model* falls apart the minute you can't keep *doing* what you *do* the way you *do* it, or the minute you don't *have* what you were used to *having.*

For example, if you work hard *doing* what you *do* – and you *have* a lot of money, marriage, a big house, and great vacations – then that makes you *be* happy, *be* loved, *be* appreciated, *be* important, *be* secure.

Now you have to keep *doing* what you *do*, to keep *having* what you *have,* to keep *being* what you're *being.* In this model, the *being* is dependent on both the *doing* and the *having*.

There is no room for getting sick, losing your job, or your spouse divorcing you because all your happiness, love, and worth is dependent on those other things you either do or *have.*

Then there is the *Have-Do-Be* model.

Most people believe if they *have* more time, more money, or more success, they are able to *do* more. Specific things – like start a new career, get married, buy a new home, travel around the world – would allow them to *be* happy, secure, loved, appreciated and fulfilled.

The reality is *having* does not produce *being-ness; being-ness* produces all of it: the *doing* and the *having*.

The starting point is to *be* happy, secure, worthy, appreciated, and fulfilled within yourself first, and that will create the *doing-ness* that is necessary to produce what you want to *have*.

Think of it this way, all the things you want to *have* are symbols of a certain kind of experience you are seeking or yearning for. However, having those things can't produce the *being;* it produces a temporary feeling that soon fades away.

For example, most people want to *have* more money, which symbolizes being free, secure, relaxed, confident, or powerful.

Some people want to *have* a relationship, which symbolizes *being* loved, connected, appreciated, acknowledged, secure, worthy, or adored.

The *doing* and the *having*, no matter which order they are in, produce a temporary feeling. Why? Feelings are short-lived.

So, the minute there is no money, you feel trapped, insecure, stressed, doubtful, and powerless.

The moment you end your relationship, you start to feel unloved, disconnected, under-appreciated, insecure, unworthy, and alone.

Have you ever noticed that as soon as the "new car" smell starts to fade, so do the feelings you once had: joy, excitement, prominent?

How about when the honeymoon phase has ended, and the chase is over in your relationship? Have you ever wondered why those butterfly feelings in your stomach have faded, leaving you to wonder how to get them back?

The framework for the *Be-Do-Have* model is built on the belief that you are a powerful and creative being.

Your power comes from your ability to make a choice, and your creativity comes from the kinds of choices you make.

When it comes to choosing, you can choose to be whomever you want, whenever you want, because all the different ways of *being* are already within you. You just have to practice accessing them, depending on which experience you desire.

You don't have to *do* anything specific or *have* anything specific to *be* a certain way.

You just BE IT.

Give up the belief that you need something external to fulfill something that is already internal.

Create the new belief that you already possess the power within you to be whomever you want, just by being it.

The biggest breakthrough of my journey was realizing the place that I am trying to get to is where I actually should be coming from.

"Come from" is used to describe your intentions. *Come from* is to originate or to be the source of.

When I *come from* being open-minded and trustworthy, my son says he feels safe enough to share with me his thoughts and ideas. He says he enjoys our conversations.

- I come from a state of inviting; therefore, people open up and share with me.

- I come from a state of playfulness; therefore, people feel safe around me.

- I come from a state of affection; therefore, people feel loved and appreciated.

Here is a chart I created to show you some of the positive payoffs when they experience you in these *Ways of Being.*

If I choose to come from a place of **being**, I receive specific payoffs:

WAYS OF BEING	**PAY OFF** **I NO LONGER NEED…**
ACCEPT MYSELF	YOUR APPROVAL OF ME
SECURE IN MY OPINION	TO ARGUE WITH YOU TO BE RIGHT
TRUSTING IN YOU	TO KEEP FINDING REASONS TO DOUBT YOU
SURRENDER WHAT I CAN'T CONTROL	TO BE STRESSED
RESPONSIBLE FOR MY PART	TO BLAME OTHERS
COMPASSION FOR YOU	TO KEEP PUNISHING YOU REPEATEDLY
PATIENT WITH YOU	TO CONTROL EVERYTHING IN YOUR LIFE
VULNERABLE WITH YOU	TO FORCE YOU TO OPEN UP TO ME
UNDERSTANDING OF THE SITUATION	TO BE ANGRY OR TRY TO FIX YOU
FORGIVING OF YOUR ACTIONS	TO HOLD ONTO RESENTMENT

Over time, I have learned to trust the way of *being* I have chosen; it will produce a series of *doing-ness* that reflects that current state of *being*. Therefore, I seldom focus on what I am going to *do* as a parent; I focus more on who my child needs me to *be* for them.

I practice this before entering a business meeting, speaking engagement, radio show, coaching session, training, or workshop, as well as I walk into my home after a long day.

I have a ritual where I stop, sit in my car or in a quiet place to center and ground myself, focus more on who I am going to *be* when I walk into a room, rather than what I am going to *do* when I am there.

After I am clear about who I am *being* – and my *come from* is aligned with my true intentions of what I am committed to creating with the people I meet – I walk into a room and *BE* it. The things I do are born out of those *Ways of Being*.

This formula allows me to *be* authentic with people and co-create our experiences together. Most of the time, I enjoy the moment, the connections, the communication, the way people respond to me, and the difference we are able to make for each other.

Love is a powerful thing, and when I'm *being* it more fully, it helps me create some extraordinary results in my life.

As promised earlier, I will share with you what I have and continue to learn from my personal journey of practicing and living by the *Be-Do-Have* model.

I have learned and continue to learn from practicing and living by the *Be-Do-Have* model that my paradigm of how I thought I should be living my life has been backward most of my life.

I realize that, in order to create my own reality as I see fit, I should start *being* there in the first place. I gain further clarity with a simple choice I make. I can call forth a state of *being* just out of the arbitrary decision to do so, giving me ultimate personal power, freedom, joy, and happiness, as much as my heart can handle.

I am learning how to *do* less and *be* more, while not in control of any of it, just consistently choosing how I want to *be* in relationship with it.

As far as *being* a dad, I am learning how to keep *being* who my adult kids need me to be for them, to continue to be the safe, loving and unconditional space for them to figure out who they are, in the rigorous pursuit of discovering their own purpose in life.

When that happens, be sure to check back with me. I will definitely write another book about that!

Now that you are gaining a better understanding of the *Be-Do-Have* model, you are better prepared to discover the other distinctions, which will be identified in other chapters. You will also experience amazing results in your relationships with your children.

Here are a few tips on how to practice *Ways of Being*:

- First, ask someone to practice with you. Make it a fun exercise with another person or a group of people, and help each other master different *Ways of Being* to help you become more effective in your relationships.

- Ask people to support you in your practice. Ask them to be patient with you as you learn to become more effective.

- Set an intention before you engage with people, like my ritual I shared with you. Find a quiet place to get yourself centered and grounded in your intention to *be,* and show up the way you want to.

- Practice teaching someone else, and you will learn at a faster pace.

- Create your personal affirmation with three distinctive *Ways of Being* that you want to master, and read it to yourself every day, all day long until you become it.

- Find yourself a *be* coach, someone you can call before you go into a meeting or before you engage with others, someone who can hold you accountable, who will help you set yourself up to win as you learn and grow.

DISTINCTION TWO
AWARENESS

It's been said that if you want to succeed big in life, you must develop a high level of emotional intelligence; also referred to as EQ, emotional quotient.

All great leaders have developed a certain level of EQ. It's the starting point to helping yourself win in life, so you can, ultimately, help others win, too.

What is Emotional Intelligence?

One of my favorite descriptions for Emotional Intelligence is having the ability to:

- Recognize, understand, and manage our own emotions

- Recognize, understand, and influence the emotions of others

One of the best descriptions for Emotional Intelligence is given by an internationally known psychologist and bestselling author, Daniel Coleman in his book, "Emotional Intelligence and Social Intelligence."

He defines Emotional Intelligence[1] as; recognizing, understanding and managing our emotions and to

---

[1] http://www.ihhp.com/meaning-of-emotional-intelligence

recognize, understand and influence the emotions of others. This means being aware that emotions can drive behavior and impact people (positively and negatively). It also involves learning how to manage such emotions - especially when we are under pressure.

Developing a higher level of EQ starts with knowing thyself through self-awareness – developing a higher sense of awareness of your thoughts, beliefs, likes, and dislikes. You must be aware of your fears, doubts, insecurities, motives, intentions, and inspiration, as well as why you make your choices.

Self-awareness is a lifestyle, something you practice every day until it becomes second nature. You must reflect deeply and notice, observe, and live in the moment.

It's not thinking from your mind but thinking within your spirit. It's a process of going within, to a certain place that is calm, still, neutral, and non-judgmental, so you can reflect and discover some things about yourself that weren't obvious before.

You're probably wondering why self-awareness is so important in parenting and how it can benefit you as a parent.

Self-awareness helps you discover more of the emotional intelligence you will need to be the best leader you can be for yourself and your family.

It helps you see the areas of improvement you need to make within yourself. You will be recognized by your kids as the person they look up to, admire, and seek for help or support.

Self-awareness helps you see some of the interpersonal dysfunctions you may be carrying with you from your past; it helps you realize that you may have brought them with you into your parenting duties.

It helps you become a more effective parent, always learning, growing and reinventing yourself.

When I think about continuously learning, growing and reinventing myself as a parent, I recall a story a good friend shared with me. Every time I read it, I am inspired to a new level.

The story comes from a great man and an amazing father, Gabriel Nossovitch. He is the co-founder of several transformational companies throughout Latin America and the United States, as well an incredible Transformational Trainer and Life Coach himself.

Gabriel's story is a great reminder that through self-awareness, parents recognize how and when to reinvent themselves in order to contribute to their children's emotional growth. I hope you receive as much value, insight, and inspiration as I do from reading it.

GIVING CHILDREN SPACE TO LEARN THROUGH THEIR OWN EXPERIENCE

By Gabriel Nossovitch

It is a beautiful Sunday afternoon. My children are playing at a neighbor's house…

But, before diving into the particular anecdote that illustrates the point I would like to make, let me provide some background.

I have two sons: Matthew and Maxim, and they are both very different. Even though they are different, they sometimes share friends. One of the shared close friends is our neighbor, Casey. This particular friend, Casey, whom they were visiting that Sunday has interests that suit both of my boys, not at the same time, but Casey; can hang with one or the other.

One of my sons, Matthew, loves video games and watching good movies. Nevertheless, he is quite an athlete and loves his cross-country team… He ran the LA Marathon at 14! On weekends, when there are no running meets, soccer games or tournaments, he would rather be home, playing with his Xbox and spending time with our dog, Martin. He calls himself a homebody. He loves being home. He feels safe there and wants to hang in his room a lot.

My other son, Max, has the "Biting red ants in his pants" syndrome. He has to always be on the move. Come the weekend, and he is getting up at 6 a.m. to go surfing with friends for a few hours, and then takes the trolley to downtown Laguna Beach to skateboard for a while. By the time he comes home in the middle of the afternoon, he is ready to raid the refrigerator and move on to play with some neighboring friends, whatever they want to do – paint, draw, skateboard or throw ball… preferably not video games or watching movies. Not his thing.

Their friend, Casey, can hang with both… Matthew and Max alike. Casey is a talented musician. He plays the piano and the cello, is an awesome video games competitor and can boogie board and surf with the best. He skateboards and throws the ball with Max or can hang for a few hours playing Xbox with Matthew.

He will sometimes be at our house and play tunes on our piano, and I know it´s in part because he knows how much I enjoy listening to him play thoroughly modern music on a rather staid Steinway. So there you have it. Casey can hang with all of us. He is a boy of many talents and has interests that he can share with whomever he happens to be spending time with – he's a really neat boy.

I remember one day when he was very young, maybe 8 or 9. He came into our house with one of my boys, and they went straight to the refrigerator and had some ice cream. I remember being annoyed that neither one of them had said hello or acknowledged my presence. I struggled with what to say… It did not feel right to directly reprimand or try to instill manners in someone else's kid. I had no idea how to deal with it… then it spontaneously came to me:

"Casey! When Max or Matthew go to your house to play… and they walk into a room where either your Mom or Dad or your siblings happen to be present… do they just walk past them or do they acknowledge them by saying hello?"

"I am not sure… why do you ask?"

"I am asking because I noticed that you did not say hello to me and ignored the fact that I was here. After noticing how it felt for me to have you walk right past me, I just want to make sure that my sons don't do that or follow your example when they are visiting your house. Will you please pay attention to how they handle themselves, and if they do that, would you remind them to acknowledge your parents or siblings if they happen to be there?"

"Yes, of course, I will be happy to." That sealed the deal with Casey for me.

I saw him a week later coming up the stairs surrounded by friends after an exhausting day of junior lifeguards training at Strand Beach. I was waiting for Max and Matthew, but they were much further back. When Casey saw me, he came over enthusiastically and said: "Hi Mister Nossovitch! It's so great to see you!" He seemed genuine and truly happy. I have never stopped appreciating Casey. He is a great kid.

Back to that Sunday afternoon. Max and Matthew are playing at Casey's house. Our house is very quiet. Suddenly I hear a boy running up the stairs, his bedroom door slam and a loud inconsolable cry. I go upstairs, open the door and find Matthew, age 9 at the time, sobbing out of control.

"Everybody hates me!" he says, "Nobody loves me." (more sobbing, big fat tears rolling down his cheeks)

"What happened?" I try to embrace him, but he pushes me away.

"Casey asked me to leave his house and go home… and Max didn't even stand up for me! He stayed there and said: Yes, Matthew! Go home; you are being really annoying and they both refused to play with me" … (sobbing harder and harder)… "They hate me! Everybody hates me! Nobody likes me!"

"Well, Matthew that is not true… we all love you. Look at the life you have! Look at all the toys and how many friends and how many teams you are on; you are very much loved. You know that!"

"Go away! You don´t understand. Everyone hates me! Nobody likes me…"

"That´s not true Matthew. We all love you. I promise you. You are very loved. Perhaps you were being annoying, but I know that Max and Casey also love you."

"Go away, Papi! You don't get it."

"No, Matthew, you are very upset, and I want you to understand how much we all love you."

"Go away!!!!"

At this point, he locks himself in his walk-in closet and holds the handle tight from the inside, so I am not able to get in. And he keeps yelling: "Go away, go away, go away."

I am truly lost. I am a coach; I teach people how to get out of undesirable states. What am I doing wrong? How can I be so ineffective with my own son? I have been helping people shift their beliefs, embrace new interpretations, etc., for two decades! What is going on here? Why am I so completely lost and confused?

So, I leave. Matthew remains locked in the closet. Half an hour. I am waiting for him to emerge. One hour. Nothing… I am getting worried. I go check on him, and he is still sobbing... I do not say anything since I figured out that he will only yell back: "Go away!"

I finally succumb and decide to call a friend. Someone who can show me what I can't seem to see right now. I call my dear friend Susan Stiffleman, who is phenomenal with children. In fact, she has written a book titled "Parenting without Struggles." She is a wonderful parenting coach for me.

I tell her the whole story.

She listened very attentively. She does not interrupt. She waits for me to finish the whole thing. I go over it again and again… she says nothing.

I am looking for validation; I am trying to be right that Matthew is being irrational, I am looking for acknowledgment that I am doing the right thing… she says nothing.

I finally dare to ask: Can you please coach me? What is it that I should be doing now? What am I doing wrong?

And she said:

"Why would you deny him his experience?"

"What?"

"Yes, you heard me… he feels rejected. He feels like nobody loves him, he feels like everyone hates him. Why would you deny him his own experience?"

"I was trying to have him see it is not true…"

"Yes, but that is your own discomfort with rejection, your own need to be included and approved... His experience is his experience. Why are you putting yours on him? Let him have his own experience!"

"Uh, WOW… I was projecting my own self?"

"At the very least, you can probably see you were not letting him have his own experience…"

"And how do I do that?"

"Let him know that you hear him, that you have empathy for how he is feeling, that his feelings are valid, that he gets to experience whatever he is experiencing…"

"You mean… I can't tell him it´s not true?"

"No! It is true for him right now! Let him have his own experience!"

And so we role played. I messed up a few times. We laughed. And then I was ready...Matthew still behind the door locked in his closet. I gently opened up the conversation:

"Matthew… you there?"

"Yes…" (sad tone)

"I just realized how awful it must be to feel that nobody loves you and that everyone hates you. And it must be so tough to feel like your brother doesn't care about you and won´t leave with you when you are asked to leave… I bet it feels really really bad, like a lump in your throat perhaps or wanting to cry a lot. I can only imagine how hard it is Matthew…"

"Yes, Papi… it hurts a lot."

At this point, the door opens gently, and he literally throws himself into my arms… cries some more for a couple of minutes. I say nothing. I just hold him. And then he lets go of me, backs up a couple of feet, looks at me with a smile and says:

"You know what? It's not true that nobody loves me. I have lots of friends and so many people who love me a lot."

You can imagine my face. I couldn't believe it. By validating his own experience, I had led him to the same conclusion that I initially intended to jam down his throat. I had been denying him the experience, trying to save him from the pain that would come. His feelings were there to teach him what he needed to learn at that moment.

He also said: "I probably need to be less bossy with them. I'm always trying to impose what I want to do, and be a little more open to doing stuff that they want to do."

I was flabbergasted. Really? The lessons were all there for him to tap into. I didn't need to force anything? Convince him of anything? Just allow the experience to be the teacher?

I left that day with a big smile on my face because I teach these things. I have been teaching about "surrendering to what is" or "being the space for something to manifest," "letting things be the way they are" and BLAH BLAH BLAH…

How could I have missed it? How could I be so dumb?

But then, I decided to give myself a break. There was no point in feeling guilty for not knowing how to be the best parent at that moment. I figured that I would probably project my own experience onto my boys many times. I also get to have my feelings and work through my shadows and trust that in allowing myself to have the experience, every moment will be packed with opportunities for growth and for serving my children in the best way that I know how. For now.

Gabriel's story paints a beautiful picture of one father's conscious attempt at figuring out how to be the father his son needs from him, at one specific moment in time.

Through his self-awareness, Gabriel realized who he was being and what he was doing now, was not supporting his son the way he needed.

I can imagine the newfound awareness Gabriel discovered, becoming the Patient, Authentic, Compassionate, and Trusting father whom Matthew desperately needed from him at that moment. He created a safe space for his 9-year-old son to be heard, validated and accepted for his own feelings.

The best way for me to become more mindful and self-aware as a father is through self-reflection.

Constantly reflecting on myself gives me the time-out I need throughout my busy days to just ponder for a moment, and look to see who I am *being* and how I might be showing up to others.

I look at them like a "half-time," which in sports is one huge opportunity to take a break, to regroup, re-evaluate what's working vs. what's not working. Then I create a new game plan based on the findings and implement it.

The more I practice, the more effective I become. At a certain point, I'm able to have my half-times at the moment in real time – no more need for pauses or timeouts. They just occur simultaneously as I am present in the moment.

I didn't always operate like this. Before my conscious awakening, I was comatose, running on automatic pilot. I was reactive, not proactive. The worst part of that entire process was my blindness to the possibility that I was unconscious and unaware.

If you had tried to point out to me that I was not self-aware or that I was unconscious to some degree, I would have thought you were crazy. I would have defended my belief and justified it with my IQ, not my EQ.

IQ is your intelligence quotient; a score derived from one of the several standardized tests designed to assess someone's individual intelligence.

From the individual intelligence, we learn, understand, and apply information to skills, logic, math skills, abstract and spatial thinking, and filter irrelevant information.

However, to create and nourish healthy, happy, and successful relationships, individual intelligence is not enough.

In order to inspire, empower, and influence others and really create extraordinary relationships, it required me to discover and develop my own emotional intelligence.

I am now discovering how to connect with others. I have a better sense of understanding, more empathy, and compassion. This is ultimately what everyone wants in their relationships, whether they know it consciously or not.

If you have not developed this part of you, it could be the difference between the relationships you currently have and the relationships you desire.

Whether or not you decide to start your journey of mindfulness, self-awareness and conscious parenting, it won't change the fact that you have some blind spots on your parenting path.

We all have them. However, the million-dollar question is:

Are you, your kids, your relationships, and the happiness you can experience together worth the risk it would take for you to believe, and embark on a new journey? A journey of your next-level of parenting?

One of the biggest heartbreaks for me is when loving, caring, and kind-hearted parents struggle and don't get the results their efforts deserve.

Often, it's because they don't know any better, or it's easier to just ignore it and hope it will fix itself.

Here is another great contribution from a young adult whom I met along my journey in the transformational world of human development.

Roxy Hernandez is 28 years old and a mother of a beautiful little boy. Roxy grew up with three older siblings. As the youngest, she felt like none of them had the patience to create a relationship with her because she felt she wasn't mature enough for them.

Roxy had a rough childhood. She felt abandoned by her parents mentally, emotionally and spiritually. Her dad was rarely home because he worked out of town seven to eight months out of the year.

When Roxy's dad was home, he drowned his sorrows in alcohol, grew depressed and made outbursts about the horrible family life he had.

Roxy's mother also was depressed and angry all the time, which led Roxy to be confused about her mom's anger, wondering if she was causing her mother so much pain.

Roxy, like most of us who experienced a dysfunctional home, held on to all of the emotional baggage from her childhood, and, potentially unaware, could have allowed some of that dysfunction to creep into her relationship with her son.

Fortunately, for Roxy, she had a transformational wake-up call, a true revelation. It was the saving grace she needed, and a real opportunity to surrender all of the emotional damage and flaws she had been carrying far too long.

The pain, guilt, resentment, self-pity, and trauma that unconsciously interfered with her parenting potential were finally being addressed.

Roxy is now a mindful, compassionate, affectionate, and patient woman on her own conscious journey of motherhood.

She is eager and excited to keep re-inventing herself so she can be the mom her son needs. She is developing her own emotional needs with an intention to raise a powerful young leader in our community.

One of Roxy's greatest gifts is her incredible insight to inspire other like-minded parents.

She wrote this letter from the perspective of her inner child. Her insight and advice came from dealing with unconscious parenting. She wants to share this insight with the intention to help parents across the world, starting with you.

I hope you can find value for yourself as you read her letter, and find the one or two golden nuggets or takeaways from this contribution. As you read the letter,

I invite you to see if you can hear your son or daughter's inner child and recognize which message they desperately want or need you to hear.

———◆———

Parents,

Please take it upon yourselves to make sure your children know how amazing they truly are. Please show them that they are a masterpiece and a beautiful creation and that in no way are they a mistake or an accident.

Please let them know constantly that you are happy, blessed, and forever grateful that you had them, and that you can't imagine your life without them.

Please teach them how to see their own value and the value in other people, to respect themselves enough to not let anyone hurt or abuse them, or to speak up if someone does.

Please Mom/Dad, never take your kids for granted and always cherish their presence, especially the times they are willing to share with you. Let them know they are worthy and deserving of all the blessings this life has to offer, not because of their accomplishments but because of the gift they are for the world.

Please hear them out even if it seems "dramatic." Their voice needs to be heard. They need to be validated. They need to know that whatever they are feeling is ok and that it matters, but most of all that it's important to you as well.

Please communicate with them with patience and tenderness. Take the time to explain whatever it is that you want or need them to learn; no matter how many times it takes, once or twice is not enough.

Please be careful not to project your own fears onto them. You don't want to ruin their courageous and fearless optimism for themselves and the world.

Please remember to take into consideration their age compared to yours. Remember they aren't wise like you. They're still learning.

Please be mindful of your anger and frustrations, making sure it doesn't spill all over them, giving them more reasons to be afraid of you.

Please empathize with them, cry with them, hold them until all of their pieces start to come back together, remembering they are whole and complete.

Please listen to them, laugh with them, and dream with them. This is what they want, and need from you the most - no lectures no criticism, just love and affection.

Please show them the value of working. Show them how to earn and achieve the goals that they have for themselves; it will build confidence and tenacity.

Please be supportive of them. Be their best champion, their biggest cheerleader, but be careful not to do it for them or enable them in any way because once they're out on their own, they'll be paralyzed with the fear of messing up, not doing it right, or not knowing how to do it at all.

Please no matter how much you like to joke around, do not say hurtful or potentially demeaning things to them. They aren't strong enough yet in their own self-love and self-acceptance to handle it.

Please acknowledge your kids and build them up so that they know how to receive compliments and praise; otherwise, they will struggle with feeling undeserving.

Please believe in them so much that they will soon learn to believe in themselves.

Please discipline them with love always, holding solid and healthy boundaries. It's ok to be firm – firm is nothing but a loving stand that one takes to teach valuable lessons.

Please instill values in them. Decide that morals, values, and principles will be the foundation to support them in their life's journey.

Please model the behavior in your own life that you expect from them, because they will surely turn out to be who you are being, and do what you are doing, if nothing changes for the better.

<hr>

As I close this chapter, I want to share some of my final thoughts about awareness and children.

When our children were born, they were born purely magnificent, fully aware, awakened, living in the present moment, curiously observing and learning.

It is through the process of the relationship they have with their families, as well as their upbringing that they begin to create their own self-limiting beliefs: doubts, fears, anxieties, and all of the other dysfunctions that intervene with who they "really" are.

It is our responsibility as parents to realize the somewhat unintentional damage we may have caused our children.

Those of us parents who get clarity on the restraints and disadvantages we may have brought upon them, unknowingly, and not to any fault of their own, we owe them.

We owe them to be and do what we can to make it right, to clean it up, to heal, to amend or to make a conscious effort to improve the quality of our parenting.

My intention is to inspire you to make a vow: to re-commit and step up to give your kids a chance to create a new relationship with you that allows you to empower and inspire them for the rest of their lives.

More importantly, when you are laying on your deathbed, I want you to be certain that you gave your kids every ounce of courage and effort.

I hope you truly see the value of becoming more self-aware and trust that there are many more blessings to come from that kind of commitment. I hope you are inspired to continue reading the rest of this book.

DISTINCTION THREE
AUTHENTICITY

When it comes to inspiring and empowering our kids, one of the most important components to parenting, is to BE authentic.

Authenticity is the process of awakening from an unconscious state of being, living in the moment, fully aware and mindful of your choice to be honest and real with yourself, forthright about your thoughts, feelings, emotions, and choices.

However, before you reach authenticity, I would like to explain to you the process you would have to be willing to go through, to be living your life authentically.

It starts with you noticing and discovering everything about your ego: What does it do? What is its purpose? How does it work? Is it affecting my relationships?

When unmanaged and unrestrained, the ego is the first mate of your ship, navigating its voyage with fear, like a pirate in the night.

Your ego pretends to be someone specific, in order for you to be liked, feel accepted, needed, appreciated, and approved of.

It interferes with your parenting potential.

Unrecognized, your ego can create fear-based conversations, narratives, or fictitious stories about yourself, your children, and the relationship you share together.

Such falsehoods can cause doubt, disbelief, anxiety, suspicion, and worry in your parenting.

That kind of parenting does not create a deep and meaningful relationship with your kids.

When you become fully aware of this transparent personality, you give yourself an opportunity to shift that context into an honest and authentic experience, opening up new possibilities to reinvent your relationship with your children.

If and when you are willing to muster up enough courage and faith and commit to reclaiming your own spirit-driven life, you will embark on your journey toward authentic living, while teaching your children by virtue of precedent.

You will also develop a solid foundation of trust that is necessary to be influential in your child's life.

Recently, I reached out to a few colleagues of mine, seeking additional perspectives and insight on this subject.

Terilynn, a Leadership Coach, wife, mother and an expert at Team Building and Personal Development, shared her thoughts.

"GET REAL"

Get real, why not? We don't get today back, so why would we spend one more moment not being real, or sharing who we authentically are?

Why would we forfeit the opportunity of not letting others know us and how we truly feel?

How could we possibly point fingers if the other person doesn't know how to show us compassion, to be a listening ear, or reach out during those times that we just need a hug?

How are they supposed to know who we really are if we wear a mask, never really letting them in?

Why do we do this?

For acceptance?

Fear of failure?

Worried about how we look?

Afraid of being vulnerable?

Maybe we are protecting ourselves, so others don't take advantage of us. Most of all, how about the lack of courage it takes to let others love us.

I say this… "Don't let another moment pass you by without getting naked with the world, being all you can be. Don't spend another second not letting people in, missing the opportunity to see your own magnificence."

God has made us all incredible and perfect.

Once we begin to embrace the gift that we are to the world, we get to come out and play; we can live life fully. Viva La Vida Grande! (Living Life Large)

I have come to know, in my 58 years on the planet that people who truly want to know us do not care about how we look. They do not care how much money we have or how smart we are. They don't care about what we do for a living or what status we have in the community.

What people want to know – is who we are deep inside.

They want to know the core of us, the essence of our being, and how to be in a relationship with us.

That is all that matters.

Have you ever wondered why kids can arrive at a new place, join a new group of other kids and just jump right in?

Why don't they stop and interview their new buddy?

I'll tell you why: They don't have time for critiquing or judging their new playmate; they just want to simply play.

They just want to have fun and enjoy the moment. They have no concern of what the other person might be thinking about them.

Do yourself a favor and take a moment to sit in a park. Close your eyes and just listen.

Listen to the chatter, hear the joy, and most of all, hear the laughter.

Why is it that we make it so complicated?

Why is it that we stop laughing?

Why is it that we hold ourselves back and possibly miss out on the best moments right in front of us?

Why do we lose our sense of humor?

Are you ready to take a look?

Are you ready to have something be different?

Are you ready to truly live?

If you are still in question, I want you to bring to mind that incredible child or children of yours. How important are they to you?

My guess is they are at the top of your list, or you would not be reading this book.

You are looking for the next level of parenting and maybe feel you have run out of ideas.

My feeling is that you already have what it takes – right inside of you.

I believe having the courage to go back deep within yourself will surface the answers that you have been looking for.

Knowing that I would be contributing to this chapter gave me the opportunity to take a moment and self-assess. I decided to get assistance from the best coaches I knew, my beautiful 12-year-old daughter "Tristen Lynn" and other teenagers.

Interview after interview, I heard a common thread amongst them all. They shared that the parents and adults who were "real" and "authentic" were the ones whom they trusted and admired. When I asked them, "How do you know they are real and authentic?" Here's their feedback:

- The adult was patient with them

- The adult was a good listener

- The adult was willing to hear their ideas

- The adult spoke from encouragement and empowerment, not correction

- The teenagers witnessed that the adult did not give up, no matter what they might be going through.

- The adult was caring and affectionate

- The adult was honest to others to their face and not back-stabbing once they walked away

- The adult was consistent in their behavior and had control over their emotions

- The adult was willing to cry if they were sad, hurt, or joyful

- The adult was willing to express their anger without rage and sadness – without blame

- The adult held them high in spite of the evidence. The young people shared that they could hear how the adult saw them in their "come from" not necessarily the words they spoke or used

- The adult stopped what they were doing at the time, looked them in the eyes and listened

- The adult was willing to admit when they were wrong or handled something incorrectly

What do you do when you feel sad or angry?

- Do you wipe and hide your tears, and pretend that nothing even bothers you?

- Do you pretend you are not angry and use passive aggressive behavior?

- Do you get quiet and or hide?

Here is some insight on that: Teenagers already know; they feel you.

They can see it in your eyes because they are observing you more intently than you are.

They want your acceptance so badly that sometimes they misbehave and lash out.

Giving your child the opportunity to see that you are real, helps them grow. It teaches them for themselves that they are compassionate and caring beings.

It gives them something to notice and focus on other than themselves.

How you handle things is key.

It is not about the fact that you may have cried or that you got angry; it's about how you resolved the conflict.

It is important to model that the conflict can be resolved, and each of us is equipped to do so.

So often, we handle everything secretly and behind closed doors, not offering any evidence that a conflict or situation can be resolved.

This often sends the message that a conflict means there is an ending coming where there is no resolution, and that can cause resentment and the feeling that their voice is not heard, implying the relationship offers no value or no solutions.

When I was growing up, my parents never allowed us, kids, to witness conflict. I didn't know they were unhappily married until they got a divorce 30 years later.

The message I got was "to hide everything and it will more than likely end."

My mother told me don't ever "bare your dirty linen in public."

"Don't ever let down your guard or you will be taken advantage of."

"Don't cry – get a hold of yourself."

"How you physically look is the key to success. It is the answer to it all. It is what matters."

"Make money, money, money, because it gives you power."

"Money will get you to the top of the chain, and you will be respected."

"Love wisely."

I am still not sure what the last one could possibly mean. To me, love is love.

So, as you can see, I learned how to be inauthentic. I did not know how to be real.

I feared trying out for sports, drama, or anything that would expose me.

I missed many opportunities. I learned not to cry and to paste a smile on my face no matter what.

People never knew I needed them. I starved myself to stay thin, and my looks became my focal point.

I spent most of the time in the mirror, learning how to manipulate people and advance by using my looks.

I worked like an addict with the goal of being financially successful. Again, I missed many wonderful opportunities.

I would wake up and wonder why no one showed me compassion or love or lent a helping hand.

I did not know how to cure loneliness. I had many broken "love" relationships because I was only halfway present, only halfway available – when my ego wasn't too busy protecting myself.

I lost my passion and my sense of humor and was in survival mode; I had truly stopped living.

Now ask yourself honestly: Did any of the above ring a bell, push a button, or make you feel sick inside?

I work with thousands of people many of those adults, parents, husbands, wives, etc.

The feedback I hear from almost all of them is, all they really wanted from their childhood was their parents' approval.

As they continue to share, more often than not, most of them still have this deep desire to be accepted and approved.

Let's face it: We all want our parents' approval; if we don't get it and it's not authentic, we spend a lifetime seeking it in other ways.

We want to know about a time that our parents were proud of us, and to hear each and every detail of what it was that made them proud.

We want to know we were important to them, that we were number one, and that we were significant.

We want them to see us and hold us as a winner, as a courageous champion.

We have the opportunity as adults and parents to have an incredible connection with our sons, daughters, and people in general.

Please don't miss your opportunity to get real and be authentic. The time is now!

As I mentioned before, we don't get today back. Change history if needed, and write your own rules. Believe in yourself, love who you are, and be willing to change the things that aren't working for you.

We all know what those are; it's just a matter of making the commitment, being disciplined and having something that matters much more than just our "stuff."

Let your kids "see" you. Let them experience you. Let them know you for the magnificent being that you are. I think that you will be pleasantly surprised at their reaction.

I must warn you though; there is a very strong chance they will be stepping forward right into your arms. They will want more and more of this kind of connection and experience; so, you better be ready.

Be proud of yourself. You have everything it takes.

Love, Terilynn

Okay, here it goes! I'm going to reveal the secret to my authenticity in the following short story.

When I was born, I was born pure spirit. Spirit knew itself to be all loving, all trusting, all accepting, of myself and others.

As I grew, I slowly forgot who I was. Ego emerged and decided to guide me for the rest of my life, vowing to always protect me and keep me safe.

I never realized that, at a certain age, I would surrender all conscious control over to my Ego, giving up all my rights to choose who I am and who I want to be.

Before I knew it, Ego had created all of these rules and put up walls to guard me and protect me from getting hurt, shielding me from the rejection and pain that comes with being in relationships.

I didn't know this was happening. I didn't know I was on autopilot, protective, defensive, and reactive.

I didn't know I was unconscious.

One day, I had a profound awakening! I was given this rare and one-of-a-kind opportunity to actually experience my own unconsciousness. I had an epiphany, and for a brief moment, I remembered just exactly who I was.

I experienced my authentic self. I remembered and felt the mighty spirit that I am, and I was profoundly moved to tears.

From that moment, I have been waking myself up from this unconscious fog, slowly and patiently reclaiming my authentic self.

Every day, I practice how to be here now, in the moment, fully present, and experiencing my experiences as I choose; to be a loving, caring, compassionate contribution to the world by shining my own light, with the intention to show my kids they also have their own light.

I encourage them to discover it for themselves, to shine it bright for the rest of the world, while realizing the light is within us all.

And the only way I can show my kids they, too, are the light is to first be willing to courageously discover and reveal myself in that process, allowing them to bear witness to it.

Here is another great example of the power of authenticity. It is the journey of a courageous single mother who thought she needed to fix her daughter.

One of my former clients, who I will refer to as Jennifer, came to me one day asking for my help.

She wanted to hire me to coach her 15-year-old daughter. Jennifer said, "I want to hire you to fix my daughter for me."

Upon the initial meeting with Jennifer, I stated that her daughter doesn't need fixing because her daughter is whole and complete.

I further explained to her that most of the behavioral issues her daughter was displaying are symptoms of an underlying issue that may be unresolved. Then, I asked her if she wanted to correct the symptom or correct the underlying issue.

Jennifer immediately replied, "I want to correct the underlying issue. I want to get to the bottom of it."

I told Jennifer it would require her to be 100% coachable and 100% committed to creating the desired results.

Once I got her commitment, I explained all her daughter really needs is a mom who can reveal her authentic self.

For the next six months, I coached Jennifer as she worked diligently to peel away parts of her ego and learn how to be open, honest and courageously revealing.

Four to six months later, Jennifer had transformed into the authentic, loving, and patient mother her daughter needed.

The transformation was the shift Jennifer's daughter was waiting for to finally feel safe to open up and share with her mom.

Sometimes, we think the issues we face are external, only to learn the biggest lessons we need to encounter lie within us.

<hr />

I recently contacted a good friend of mine, Raphael Natale, and asked him to share some insight with me. On behalf of you, I created a few questions for him to answer.

Raphael Natale is an award-winning speaker and author of the book, "The Art of Balance." He is the founder of Authentic Technologies, a Certified Human Potential Trainer and a Certified Clinical Hypnotherapist. Raphael is as authentic as they come. Below is his contribution:

What does authenticity mean to you, and what does it mean to be authentic?

I like to first go to see how the wise people in the world define things, and if you look it up, it says authenticity is to be genuine; to be real.

If you ask most people if they are authentic, they will all say yes! I am... I'm me... I'm genuine... I'm real.

The truth is most people live in a world of "should," and "have-to;" living their life according to someone else's values and expectations.

People are never really clear about their own values, and if you leave your own values unexamined, the unconscious beliefs and assumptions you possess may lead you to feel trapped in the world – trapped in your own existence. It's not your own world you'll be living in; you'll be living in everybody else's world.

You have to become aware of your own likes and dislikes, combined with your ability to trust your own motives and emotions. Most people have put their own coping mechanisms into place.

A coping mechanism is a mask.

I love the word personality because the word persona comes from the Greeks and means mask.

Everyone thinks they are their personalities that their personalities are their authentic selves, but that is far from the truth.

The mask is only used to hide their vulnerable true self because the ego is afraid of your ability, but the mask is worn in a daily and exhaustive attempt for acceptance and to please others.

People are faced with a choice between living with the possibility of rejection, which nobody wants or the true self.

People would rather have occasional praise for the inauthentic superficial masked self, and it's always the inauthentic self that wins, because of the ego's overwhelming desire for praise and approval.

The ego doesn't like the authentic self.

It's actually the antithesis of the real self because there; you are non-conforming, non-materialistic, self-aware –

a unique individual more affected by your own possibility than what other people think about you.

It's about learning how to trust your own self-knowledge, which is acquired from a willingness to observe and assess everything you are being and doing.

It's like taking an honest inventory of your likes, your dislikes, your weaknesses, and your strengths.

Taking personal inventory can be a daunting, very painful task because it's not always pleasant to face the truth, but most of us avoid it at all cost.

However, as uncomfortable as it may be, it's the key to living your authentic life.

When you put in the work, you think it's hard, but the rewards far outweigh the work you put in. When you're putting in the work, you think it's the most difficult road to travel because growth is painful. Growth takes energy to really push yourself.

Like a little plant, it has to push its way through the ground in order to get to the light.

Sometimes growth is painful, but when you get to the other side of it, you realize it was worth it because by living authentically, you are true to your values.

In my line of work, I call it being your gift. That has nothing to do with your talents or what you have learned. It's more about how you are expressed.

You are expressed by the creator in a certain way, and everybody is so unique that nobody is expressed in the same way.

Authenticity is your true form, and function follows form. When you're authentic, the functions actually come to support your purpose in life, and your purpose in life is to be yourself and come from love.

I feel like I am authentic. How would I know if I really am?

Listen to your deepest feeling of who you really are. This is distinctively different from who your ego wants you to be.

To know your authentic self, you must also know your ego.

To know your ego is a feeling, or an urge to try to get something you feel is missing from within yourself – a compulsivity.

Compulsivity is defined as: "I must do, I must have."

When you are truly authentic, you don't need anything from anybody. You don't need anything from outside of yourself. You just are, and you are more freed up, willing to give more.

Authenticity comes from a feeling of peace and love, and I think everybody knows that distinction, but of course, the ego will do everything in the world to stop you from coming from that place, because the ego is linked to your survival context.

Let me give you a metaphor.

If you and I were swimming and I pushed your head down under the water, how hard would you fight to get back to the surface for air? I'm sure you would fight pretty hard to get back to the top of the water to breathe.

That's the actual drive the ego has when it's triggered. It has you locked into automaticity, into your automatic, pre-programed survival driven behaviors.

It takes some real work to break that kind of drive, to understand its mechanism and how to dismantle it. You can dismantle it to a certain point, but you still need it. Why? A tree could fall on your head, so you need it to help you get out of the way of that falling tree.

That's the ego saying: Get out of the way; there's danger ahead.

So, its job is to save your life, but under the guise of saving your life, it destroys your life because it never helps you to live your authentic self to be in that space of peace and love.

So, knowing you are authentic comes down to a feeling, a feeling of wanting more to give rather than to get.

I think that's what it means in the Bible when Jesus says if you are willing to lose your life, you find your life.

When you are willing to give, you aren't worried about yourself anymore. So, in a sense, you have lost your life, and you are only caring about other people.

What are the benefits to becoming authentic?

To live a life of peace and love, there is no stress – that's for sure. There's only health, freedom, and happiness.

Hinduism talks about karma. Here in America, we say what comes around goes around and giving and receiving in the same wheel.

When you are authentic, you are just out there being you, sharing your gifts with other people. You're in a giving mode. The only thing that can happen is that it comes back to you.

You just relax, be yourself, and everything you want is given to you. It's the strangest thing in the world; I don't know even if Einstein could have explained how it works.

You get lighter, develop a better sense of humor, and don't take things so seriously or personally.

By being authentic, you discover your life's purpose, your mission, why you have the talents that you have, and why you love and appreciate the things you do.

Now that I know how to be authentic, I don't even work anymore. I just get up and Be me every day, and I make a lot of money being and doing that.

Don't ask me how because I don't know how the money, love, and support just keeps coming.

That's what I'm putting out authentically into the world. The only place it can be coming from is back to you.

How can me "being" authentic empower and inspire my children?

Children learn by two methods, reinforcement and modeling. We are so brilliant as children. We are like sponges, absorbing everything.

We are so smart when we are young that we just look at our parents and decide, "That's how I want to be." We model them.

We act and behave just like they are acting and behaving, and then we reinforce it. We do it over and over again, and then it becomes us.

So, by being authentic, you are being the best role model you can be.

The biggest mistake parents make is wanting to be friends with their kids. You can't be friends with them, you "gotta be" their parent.

Your mission is to put out a good product into the world, and by the time they are 18 to 25 years of age, your job is done.

So, how would you being authentic empower and inspire your kids?

It's going to make them have a wonderful life because they are going to have a role model whom they can trust, who is peaceful, loving and caring. That's what you are going to teach them – not by telling them but by being who you truly are.

<hr>

After working with teenagers for over 20 years, what they want most from their relationships with their parents is to have a safe, honest, open and authentic space to share themselves wholeheartedly; without judgment, ridicule, disapproval, and discord.

When I'm in the training room working with teenagers, what they share with their group is anything short of an awe-inspiring tribute to their own truth.

They are dying for you to be real with them, to open yourself up to them, to stop pretending you have all the answers, to be honest enough to admit your fears, doubts, and faults.

They share that they desperately want you to figure out who you really are and just be that. Then your children can put down their walls, their shields, and their coping mechanisms to trust you again and start learning how to be who they really are – to start living a beautiful and authentic life.

Here are a few suggestions on how to start living authentically. Keep in mind these are not definitive answers, only suggestions. Each of you will have different starting points.

- Start with therapy, depending on where you are in your life's journey. For some, therapy is a good place to start to surrender some of the residual pain you may still be carrying with you from your past. Therapy is an excellent way to be self-aware and heal yourself.

- You may also start with meditation because it offers multiple benefits such as stress reduction, improving concentration, increasing self-awareness, and happiness.

- Some people seek a Life Coach to help them access more of their full potential, gain clarity of goals; help improve their communication, better understand circumstances and solutions; and help find passion, purpose and inner peace.

- Launch your journey in Transformational Training to gain personal freedom by helping you complete your past, tapping into self-love and/or personal power. Your journey will help you discover your authentic self and live peacefully while finding your passions and purpose.

Techniques:

- Acknowledge your ego, its fears, and its doubts, as well as the games it plays to keep you guarded, protected, and cynical. Be honest with your observations, and share them with someone you trust to witness new insight. The more you notice, the more conscious you become, and the more you are able to correct your abilities.

- Relinquish all needs to define yourself and to be understood by others. Surrender the game of trying to be someone specific for the world: to be appreciated, validated or liked by them. Just be you. Have fun, lighten up, enjoy yourself more, be more playful, and stop being serious all the time.

- Work on your spirituality. According to Ryan T. Howell, Ph.D., in an article for Psychology Today, (posted February 27, 2013) entitled, "Why Be

Spiritual? Five Benefits of Spirituality" demonstrates that spiritual people are gracious, optimistic, compassionate, and self-actualized. They manifest positive emotions such as optimism, generosity, and compassion. Spiritual people also have happy and positive relationships, high self-esteem, greater meaning, and purpose in life.

DISTINCTION FOUR
PATIENCE

A man observed a woman in the grocery store with her 3-year-old daughter inside the shopping cart. As they passed the cookie section, the little girl asked for cookies, and her mother told her no. The little girl immediately began to whine and fuss. The mother quietly said,

"Now Monica, we just have half of the aisles left to go through; don't be upset. It won't be long."

Soon they came to the candy aisle, and the little girl began to shout for candy. When told she couldn't have any, the little girl began to cry. The mother said,

"There, there, Monica, only two more aisles to go, and then we'll be checking out."

When they arrived at the checkout stand, the little girl began an outcry for gum and burst into a tantrum upon discovering no gum would be purchased. The mother patiently said,

"Monica, we'll be through this checkout stand in 5 minutes, and then you can go home and have a nice nap."

The man followed them out to the parking lot and stopped the woman to compliment her.

"I couldn't help noticing how patient you were with little Monica," the man said.

The mother replied,

"I'm Monica ... My little girl's name is Tammy."

-Author Unknown

I found this story on the internet. I love this story so much because Monica knew, to help her daughter deal with not getting what she wanted, it would require an enormous amount of patience from her.

It also shows Monica was wise enough to know that resisting her daughter's behavior would have further perpetuated the acts.

In psychology circles, there's a common saying: "What you resist, will persist. What you embrace, dissolves."

In this story, Monica understands she cannot let herself be caught up in psychological resistance to her daughter's outcries and temper tantrums.

If Monica exerts her resistant energy toward her daughter's negative behaviors, both Monica's energy and her daughter's energy will prolong and continue to feed her daughter's negative behavior.

Monica was wise enough to know the only way she could keep herself from being in resistance to her daughter's tantrums and feeding the dysfunction, was to practice the art of patience. She let the tantrum run its natural course until it slowly died out on its own.

For me, mastering my ability to be patient in my parenting is one of the most important components to building emotional stability in my children.

Patience as a way of being is a powerful yet silent energy that our kids need from us, to grow and develop a strong sense of self and purpose.

Such development and purpose instill the confidence young people need to navigate the extraordinary challenges they will face in today's world. Because our kids do not yet know who to be or how to do this for themselves, it will be up to us, the parents to create a safe space for them to discover, develop, and grow – to become the competent leaders we want them to be.

When you think of wise teachers, they all seem to possess an innate ability to be calm, still, and patient with us, as we learn from them and from ourselves. They don't react. They don't resist. They don't panic. They just are this thing called patient.

You too have this ability. You just need to discover it for yourself – and practice, practice, practice – so you can be that wise teacher for your kids.

Now, let's explore more about the distinction called patience.

Patience is developing the ability of not necessarily needing it right now and trusting that it will come; when it is meant to materialize. Later, I will explain in more detail.

For now, let's just say, as human beings, we are instinctually hard-wired to satisfy our needs whenever we are able to: as soon as I possibly can, but preferably right now.

Then the fear creeps in, doubting that you will get another chance, and if it doesn't happen now, it may never happen. The fear is what makes us go into a desperate mode of need, to want to get it immediately. Such compulsivity and desperation make us impatient in our parenting.

That kind of energy causes us to be tense, edgy, nervous and stressed.

Stress turns to worry, and worry turns to anxiety when we do not know when, how, or why.

When we are in a constant hurry, we get frustrated. "It's not the way I want it!" We ask, "How long is it going to take?"

It is similar to when kids ask during a long road trip: "Dad, are we there yet?"

Parenting from this place is unhealthy. It sabotages your

ability to contribute your wisdom and your advice to help your kids acquire success. Your messages and insight get lost in translation when you deliver it impatiently. They can't hear you, and more importantly, they can't hear the message you want to be delivered. Being impatient gets in the way of your ability to "show up" to your kid as the calm, assured and, the confident leader they need you to be.

A few years ago, my wife brought a dog trainer into our home to teach our family how to train our two dogs. What we didn't understand was that the dog trainer was there to train us, the humans.

The trainer demonstrated that when our dogs had nervous, anxious, and excited energy, they could not hear us or follow any of our commands.

It was to our advantage that we learn how to relax and calm our energy, shifting our way of being, to be patient and at ease, so the dogs could relax and calm their energy. When that was achieved, our dogs followed our directions like a magic spell! It was a validation that kids, teens, and adults respond to our personal way of being.

Patient energy is one of the most powerful and influential energies essential for positive parenting, according to the American Society for the Positive Care of Children, in an article (posted March 12, 2014) entitled, "Top 10 Positive Parenting Tips."

From city to city, and training room to training room, I consistently hear teenager's express desperation for their parents to *be* patient with them. They don't always know exactly how to articulate it so powerfully and eloquently, but below are some examples of the messages they want you to know. I will translate the "teenglish" for you.

⸻ ◆ ⸻

- I want my parents to walk alongside me, as I make mistakes, advising me calmly and more compassionately.

- I want my parents to understand how hard it might be for me, to put themselves in my shoes without getting angry or upset.

- I want my parents to create a safe, loving and peaceful environment for me, so I can be open and honest, without them overreacting or jumping to conclusions.

- I want my parents to be that centered, grounded and optimistic person (my rock) I can see when I'm nervous or scared.

- I want my parents to show me how to deal with issues calmly, instead of the reactive, fearful, panic mode they always show.

- I want my parents to control their emotions and encourage me while pointing out the things I need to change or correct.

- I want my parents to believe I will arrive at my destination on my own time, not within their timeframe or when they want it.

These are a few of the cries I have heard from teens who become vulnerable enough and feel comfortable enough to open up and share what they desire from their parents.

Of course, they won't share this with you. They will put a smile on their face and act as though everything is fine. Isn't that the true signature of a child or teenager?

It is the wise parent who can honestly assess him/herself and recognize what is missing in their ability to be more patient and to make the necessary adjustments.

This is not to say you are not patient parents. It's just to open a possibility of a higher level, a deeper understanding and a broader ability to *be* the patient mom or dad your kids need from you.

Each child or teenager is different, so this is not a

formula for all children. It's a starting point for you, to see what adjustments you may need to make for your own children.

Let's remember, as parents, we are teaching our kids how to be patient through our ability to master this art form, as we learn how to deal with our own challenges.

"Patience is the calm acceptance that things can happen in a different order than the one you have in mind." - *David G. Allen*

This is one of my favorite quotes about patience because it reminds me, no matter how much I want something to look or happen, I have no control over any of it, leaving me only with a choice to accept it or not.

When you learn how to be truly patient with your family, what you inherently are saying to them is: "*I respect you, and what it is you are going through.*"

The statement you ultimately make to them when you are patient is: *"I am not going to take things personally, and I trust that the outcome will be assured, no matter what course it takes."*

When your patience is authentic and obvious, it is a declaration of your support for them. It says: *"I want you to be happy. Therefore, I will help you figure things out, no matter how long it takes."*

A few years ago, I was at a charity event with some of the young people from my latest teen training. We were there to help rebuild a home for a military veteran.

My team and I wore t-shirts displaying my logo, and someone asked aloud: "Who is Alex Urbina?"

I said to the man: "I am."

The man looked at me and said: "What qualifies you to be a leader?"

I responded: "I have made many mistakes in my life."

The man looked at me and smiled.

One of the biggest mistakes I made early on in my parenting journey still affects me emotionally.

My wife and I had children while in our late teens. I was quite immature and impatient as a father.

In my unconscious state of parenting, I didn't realize my lack of patience could be so detrimental to the emotional growth of my children.

It wasn't until my mid-30s, about 10 years after I embarked on my journey of consciousness and better parenting, that I noticed something about my younger self, which broke my heart.

It was a profound moment that left a lasting impression and forever changed my life.

One weekend, I transferred all of our family movies from VHS to DVD. The kids were so anxious to watch them. "Dad, can we watch them when they are done?"

Finally, on Sunday night, I told the kids we could watch the DVDs, so they excitedly selected one for all of us to watch.

There we were – my wife, my son, my two daughters and me – watching what I thought was going to be a happy moment as we reflected on some glorious times.

One section of the DVD replayed a moment when my wife, my three kids, my father, who later passed away, and I were on a fishing trip.

My dad was fishing on his own. My wife was sitting on the floor with my two little girls, videotaping me as I prepared my fishing pole.

My 9-year-old son was fishing next to his grandpa, and as he reeled in his line, it was tangled.

In the next scene, I watched my 9-year-old son walk up to me with his tangled fishing line, asking me to help him.

In his own frustration and disappointment, he innocently looked at me to be that loving, patient, and gentle father who needed to simply say: "Sure no problem. Come here and let me show you again how to untangle your line."

Who I was for him, instead, was a frustrated, disappointed, and immature young man, who was impatient and intolerable.

"How did you do that?" I responded. "Weren't you paying attention? I thought I taught you how to fish."

As I try to type these words to explain to you the look on his face, tears are running down my face. I become choked up and sad every time I think of it or tell this story.

However, it's a good story to tell because, during that moment, I realized I was unable to provide my son what he needed from me.

I was too unconscious and living on automatic pilot. I was too immature, arrogant, and selfish to know differently. There was more interpersonal growth needed on my part to be that loving, patient, and encouraging father that most of us dads strive to be.

The wise 45-year-old man now sitting here sharing this story with you wishes he can go back and teach the younger immature father some life lessons.

I wish I could go back and explain to him what that little boy needed was the patient, calm, compassionate, and understanding old man who he would later become.

However, I can't. I can't go back and correct anything. So after the heartbreak, the tears, and the emotional release of realizing how damaging that may have been to my little boy, I grabbed his hands at the age of 17 and apologized, asking him to forgive me.

I reminded him that he was an amazing son and that every time I was angry or frustrated at him during his childhood wasn't his fault. It was his dad's insecurities.

That day I made a commitment to him and my daughters that I would practice being more patient with them – to never let my frustrations, fears, and, insecurities be projected onto them.

I asked them to hold me accountable and to call me out whenever I was unaware.

Sometimes, we need to be humble enough to acknowledge our weaknesses not so much for us but for our kids. At the end of the day, they pay the price while we learn how to master ourselves in our lifetime.

We as parents are always aware of the way we manifest ourselves to our children. Unconsciously, we might be doing more harm to their emotional growth than actually contributing to it.

Two of my good friends, Wendy and Joey Amara, are conscious parents with three beautiful babies. Wendy is an amazing wife, extraordinary mother, and a seasoned life coach in her practice.

Joey is a loving and patient father. They are great examples of patient parents. I have asked them to contribute their insight on the art of being patient. Here is their contribution:

Being patient to me means to be present, and in the moment, 100% focused on what's happening here and now in front of me.

Realizing that, with whatever is happening right now in my life, everything is okay. Everything that I want to show up in our life is going to come. It just may not come at the exact second I want it to appear.

Being patient means waiting for it to unfold in the universe's timeline, not my timeline, or the way I think the timing should pan out; it means living on the universal clock.

In our society, we want everything quickly, and we want to jump from one thing to another. Let's face it; we live in a fast food nation.

Being patient is a state of being.

Learning to be patient to me means learning to go with the flow because there are certain things I have no control over.

What helps me practice patience is taking a deep breath, when I'm in the moment, and realizing I am not in control. I chose to just let things be the way they are.

Of course, I'm still wearing the parent hat, and I'm still the leader in the family dynamics. However, the kids have their own agenda and their own plan. Things often work out better, most of the time, when I just go with the flow of what is happening in the family, instead of being ridged and trying to make it look my way.

When I choose to go with the flow of what's happening in the family, it often leads to a calmer more peaceful environment. Things don't always work out the way I had planned them. That's ok because it's part of the process of surrendering and going with it.

The moment I surrender control, patience becomes easier for me, by letting go of the need to have it look the way I want it to when I want it to.

One of the benefits of being patient is I get to discover a lot more information about my children than I could otherwise. If I rush through the moment or try to control that moment, there are things I won't notice about my kids that are extremely important to me as a parent.

When I'm being impatient, I cannot see the warning signs my kids are revealing to me. Impatience often times creates tension in the relationship and doesn't allow much space for vulnerability.

When we are being impatient, we focus more on the doing because we are in the midst of wanting something to happen that is not currently happening. Whether it is a feeling or an event, we want it to happen more than we want what the moment is trying to teach us or reveal to us.

Some of the benefits of being patient are noticing things I would not have noticed before. I notice my kids' feelings and what my kids are saying, as well as what they are not saying. It creates moments of true connection – a deeper and more meaningful connection.

Being patient with my kids is an opportunity to be fully connected to my kids, and I love that.

Being patient is accepting the way things are in each moment and allowing the process to unfold the way it does in its own time, not necessarily yours.

Patience to me is an art form, requiring practice from us parents.

When you are willing to let go of the "resistance," or the inner struggle of needing or wanting the desired result when you want it, you will be liberated to create new outcomes.

Let's review my son's tangled fishing line as an example. In this scenario, I recognize I was in resistance to fixing his pole because I wanted to prepare my own pole and start fishing myself.

I was in resistance to accepting that my son is only 9 years old and is not a seasoned fisherman. He is going to make mistakes because that's what 9-year-olds do.

I was also in resistance to not accepting that we had plenty of time to fish.

I was in resistance to seeing and embracing a new opportunity for another teachable moment: to show my son how to fix his own line, no matter how many times it would take for him to learn.

I was also in resistance to realizing that fishing is not always about catching fish, but it is also about bonding, connecting, sharing, teaching, learning, loving, laughing, and creating memorable moments together.

As you practice patience, you eventually move into a state of understanding that life is always unfolding on its own timeline.

Here is a great example: When you are in bumper-to-bumper traffic, impatient and frustrated, how do I know with certainty that you are meant to be stuck in traffic?

I will give you a few seconds to think of an answer.

One, two, three. OK, the answer is because "you are."

When you are stuck in traffic, ask yourself this question: How do I know I am supposed to be here right now? The answer: because I am.

If you weren't meant to be stuck in traffic, you wouldn't be; you would be somewhere else.

Surrender to the fact that you can't be somewhere else other than where you are in each moment. When things happen in your life that you don't want, don't like, or are in resistance to, ask yourself: How do I know this is meant to be happening right now? BECAUSE IT IS!

Remember, the universe has its own plan and timeline. Whether you like it or not, whether you agree with it or not, your job is to not resist it, but ask yourself: OK, now what? What do I want to do now? Where do I want to go from here?

All things happen for a reason. If you haven't learned that yet, hopefully, you will soon.

From my experience, my impatience blinds me from being present, living in the moment, and trusting that all things really do happen for a reason, even when the reason is not crystal clear to me or doesn't make sense.

I hope you have comprehended a common theme in this chapter: trust.

Patience is a high level of trust. Some may call it faith, which is often described as the confidence or trust in someone or something without proof.

Start believing all things work out for the best even when in the moment, it doesn't look like it. Do this consistently until you start witnessing the results.

When you create enough results, you will relax more, and a higher level of patience will emerge from within.

I am a big believer in a world of unlimited possibilities, which motivates me to create new results for myself.

Impatience will almost always sabotage my ability to recognize possibilities for new solutions that may be trying to reveal themselves to me.

More often than not, being impatient robs me from seeing the bigger picture, from seeing how I can make a greater difference or a greater impact.

The next time you find yourself being impatient, ask yourself: What is the lesson for me to learn at this moment? What different possibility can I create from this moment with what's before me?

"When life gives you lemons, make lemonade" is a proverbial phrase used to encourage optimism and a positive can-do attitude in the face of adversity or misfortune.

Below is the motto I use for inspiration during moments of adversity:

"It is what it is, so what! Now what? If it's to be, it's up to me."

The motto encourages me to create something new or different from the current results. Let's remember we cannot empower or inspire anyone if we manifest impatient energy.

How patience benefits children:

- They are calm, relaxed and focused on solutions

- They are optimistic and hopeful

- They learn to trust themselves and their efforts

- They are more comfortable connecting with you to build a better relationship

- They are more motivated to improve their skill sets

- They are more likely to weigh the pros and cons before rushing a decision

- They achieve goals, stay the course, and pay their dues

Impatience disempowers and repels your children, causing them to turn away from you.

It is a common notion that the elderly have a soft, gentle calmness about them that kids love and need. That kind of tranquility makes people feel relaxed, safe and, secure.

To me, it's their wisdom – not that they are elderly.

I want you to learn how to create this kind of context within yourself to foster healthy growth and development for you and your family.

What I don't want you to hear is patience means giving up, doing nothing, or sitting back and letting things fall out of the sky. Patience isn't giving up. It's giving in to the idea that it has to be or should be, right now.

Some of the benefits your kids will experience from your ability to be more patient is a certain level of trust that will develop within your relationship.

Your children will surely feel safe enough to reveal and share more with you, creating a more meaningful connection between you and them – a special bond serving as the foundation to empower and inspire them as your relationship advances.

The environment in which our children are raised influences their ability to grow and develop in a healthy way. This energy we cannot see but can feel is an important component of that healthy environment they need to develop in.

How patience benefits parents:

- Learn to be more cooperative, empathetic, reasonable, and forgiving

- Reflect and gain clarity to best support your children

- See new possibilities you cannot see when you both are impatient

- Learn to better adapt, overcome challenges, and to persevere

- Draw your teens to you, rather than away from you

- Discern what's effective and ineffective with your parenting style

- Model and teach your kids to be more patient with themselves and others

- Gain a better understanding about your teenager: their motives and their needs

- Experience more positive energy

- Allow you to see some of the warning signs or course corrections you need to make with your kids

A Few Lessons or Activities to Practice in the Art of Being Patient:

Activity #1 - Instead of taking your car to work today, get up early and take the bus or the commuter train, and as you sit there waiting at the bus stop or train station, practice not thinking of anything. Turn your mind off, and sit there waiting quietly and peacefully, as you resist nothing and control nothing.

Activity #2 - Choose one day out of the week to drive the speed limit, never exceeding it – not one mph faster than posted on each street or highway.

Activity #3- Notice all the shortcuts you take, and make more of an effort to take a long way around instead of choosing the easiest route.

In order to create a new habit of being patient, slowing down your fast-paced lifestyle, you might want to take the stairs instead of taking the elevator to different floors. If you like to check in to your flights early to get a faster boarding time, check in later, patiently boarding the plane. When you are in line at the grocery store, allow others to go in front of you from time to time, to train yourself to be more patient.

Bonus Homework:

Buy a puzzle or a game of checkers and invite your teenager to sit and participate with you. Tell them it's your homework to learn how to be a better parent. If they ask you why, tell them it's to practice being more patient.

As you and your child partake in the activity, I invite you to practice creating patient energy within yourself. Practice turning off your mind. Cease or shut down all of your racing thoughts, ideas, worries, and concerns, and let yourself be in the present moment – your patient energy connecting with their patient energy.

Ask open-ended questions, but spend more time listening than speaking. For example, you may ask: Do you have anything fun planned next weekend? If there was one thing you could adjust in my parenting, what would it be? Why?

Before you go to bed later that night, journal your experience by writing what you learned, and identify any a-ha moments.

Learn now how to master being more patient in your life so you can teach your kids how to master it for themselves. Your kids learn from your example, behaviors, and practices more so than what you verbalize.

Enhance your ability to *be* patient, and your children will trust you at a level that far exceeds anything you can ever *do* to earn their trust.

DISTINCTION FIVE
PRESENT

To be present is to be fully accepting the current moment in time as it is actually happening, without any racing thoughts, worries or fears. It is the art of being here now.

Having the honor of being the father of two beautiful, loving, and compassionate daughters have changed me and my life in ways I could never have imagined.

My two girls have taught me more about who I am, and what I'm truly capable of in my life than 10 lifetimes combined. They are my greatest teachers, and I am truly grateful for them.

Witnessing their journey is one of the greatest gifts from God. Since the moment they were born, I have discovered things about myself I would not have done otherwise.

They are responsible for a significant part of my transformation. Because of my deep love for them, I discovered my own heart, tapped into my own vulnerability, and shared with them wholeheartedly, in order to closely connect with them.

As they grew into teenagers, they weren't always forthcoming with me about how they felt or their experiences.

So, it forced me to look closely, to pay attention, and to really learn how to be present: intently observe them, notice the small openings for me to engage, and to be there for them when they need me.

When they were young, being present didn't seem to be as daunting and as challenging as it appears to be in today's world, since we didn't have as many distractions.

The 21st Century has brought us a whole new world of technology that has overstimulated us to some degree, as well as generated an enormous amount of distractions: sitting in front of our computers for hours on end, constantly checking our cell phones, or responding to numerous emails.

Now add all of those external distractions combined with the laundry list of internal distractions we have created within our own minds, such as thinking about things from the past or what I need to do in the future, or worrying about this or worrying about that. Before we know it, we are more checked out in our lives than checked in.

You can easily find yourself no longer in the moment and experiencing life as it is occurring, being more focused on other things that have little to no value or importance to you.

Because you are reading this book, I would guess what's most important to you is focusing your attention on connecting with the people you love most in your life: your family.

Your kids are yearning to connect with you, too. When they are young, they won't have a problem telling you they want it, but that only lasts up to a certain point – the point they give up on asking you, with nothing in return.

They may give up on asking you, but they will never stop seeking your attention or needing your approval in other ways.

I want to share with you this heartfelt story I found online about a man named David Rosenman and his 9-year-old daughter. It reminds me how easily we can forget, as a parent, that our kids really need us to be present and living in the moment with them.

Dear Fellow Human Beings,

This morning, at her request, I took our 9-year-old daughter to a coffee shop. She brought with her a little crocheting activity; I brought the newspaper, a notebook, pen, and my phone.

This was going to be an outing not unlike others we'd had before: While sitting at the same table, we'd do our own things — she'd keep herself occupied with something, and I'd catch up on emails, organize my week, get work done, etc.

Sound familiar?

Today, she made one additional request: "Daddy, can you not read the paper or doodle or check email today? Can we just be together?" I'm not trying to be melodramatic; that was her question.

So today, we were together. She showed me her yarn project. I recalled the day she was born. We compared notes about whether or not couples at other tables were on "dates." (She likes to impersonate people on dates — resting her smiling face on her hand and practicing a starry-eyed stare).

She told me about her friends and their hamsters. I watched her chew her breakfast sandwich and melted a little bit as I thought about how much I love her.

I wished it hadn't taken her past experience and her courageous reaching out for me to give her the attention she so wanted and needed.

Before we left, I went up to the counter to order a take-out snack for her brother. When I returned to our table, there was a note, left face-down, in front of my seat.

My daughter told me that a woman, before leaving the coffee shop, had asked her if I was her father and said that the message was for me.

I looked around – nobody was there – and flipped over the paper to find the words below.

I work at a school where many daughters don't have fathers & those who do have never in their lives have him watch & listen & devote 100% of his attention to her for as long as you did on one Sunday morning. You have no idea what a gift you are giving to all the teachers who are responsible for educating her from now until she graduates.

This anonymous message was enough of a reinforcement for me, and I hope more people might be guided by its power and by its author's thoughtfulness.

Please don't wait for your child or other loved ones to plead for your attention like mine did — he or she might not.

Expect that no one will leave a note for you — such beauty in this world is far too rare. I invite you to share the gift of this experience with me: Choose to be present today — even for just a little while — for someone you love. If you see it happen somewhere, consider leaving a note — it sure does leave an impression. – David

Being present, simply put, is allowing yourself to experience your experiences at the moment, in "real time," as it's actually happening.

Sometimes in our lives, we find ourselves there in the moment while "it's" happening, but we are not present. We are not experiencing "it."

When I am with someone I have created permission to coach, I will ask them: "How are you feeling?" Their response quite often back to me is: "Good."

I explain to them that good is not a feeling or an experience and ask them to check back into the present moment to observe or notice what they are currently experiencing.

Could it be possible that we as human beings are not *being* anymore? We are not experiencing our experiences or feeling our feelings?

Could it be possible that we can be witnessing life as it unfolds, but in our head, we're having multiple thoughts about what we are seeing and no longer experiencing the moment?

I saw a picture on the internet a few months ago of an elderly woman enjoying an event. The image appears to capture what looks like her enjoying the moment, being fully present and fully engaged; it put a smile on my face.

The photo depicts an elderly woman leaning on a street barrier, gazing onto the red carpet at a premiere in Hollywood, California. The look on her face is priceless as she appears to be star struck while gazing at her favorite celebrity.

All around her are about forty people all holding up their cell phone cameras taking pictures or videos of what she seems to be fully experiencing there in the moment. None of the other people have expressions that can match the joy on her face and what appears to be a magical moment and a day that this lady will never forget.

I have heard many thought leaders describe being present as stepping out of your "thinking mind" and coming back to the actual experience that is happening in the moment.

They say that when we step into our thinking mind, we lose contact with our personal reality.

Quite often I work with people who have analytical-style personalities, and when it appears they have checked out of the present moment, I ask them: "Where did you go?"

After we both share a laugh, most of them tell me they go into their mind, trying to figure out what's going to happen next.

Could it be that – when we are too busy thinking about what's going to happen next, trying to figure what to do next, or focusing on how to handle a possible situation that hasn't even occurred yet – we miss what is actually happening now?

Deepak Chopra once said, "It isn't necessary to know anything in advance."

However, why are we so fascinated with wanting to know?

Imagine what your life would look like – what your relationships would look like – and what it would feel like if you gave up all the necessary urges or longing to know what's going to happen next?

When I finally surrender the need to know or anticipate what's going to happen next, I feel free, peaceful, relaxed, present, and joyful in the moment and all that it has to offer me. When I am present, I am happy and full of love.

In Buddhism, when it comes to being present, you will hear the term mindfulness, which is the practice of being present with what is, not trying to be in a different moment.

What our children want and need from us, is to *be* paying attention to them on purpose, in the present moment, without judgments.

When you are able to *be* this for them, you mirror their existence. You allow them to know they matter to you, and they are important to you, to be validated by your presence.

You being present for them and with them is like saying, "I see you."

Being seen or recognized in a single moment is one of the greatest gifts you can give someone.

It is commonly said that the worst form of punishment is to ignore someone.

In some tribal communities, if you have broken the law, the tribe wouldn't necessarily hurt you physically as your punishment but stand together and ignore you for the entire day.

Depending on the severity of the crime, they might ignore you for a week or for months.

When you are ignored, it means you don't exist. We as human beings have this great need for attention, for approval, to be validated, to know that "I am here."

Recently, I heard someone say people would prefer for you to say something negative or hurtful to them than for you to ignore them.

How many times in a day have you ignored someone?

Whether it was intentional or not? Whether you were aware of it or not?

How many times do you walk by your kids in the hallway at home and, at the very least, don't even make eye contact with them? You don't say "hello" or "good morning," or "you look beautiful today."

Imagine if every time you walked by your kids and didn't either make eye contact with them or smile at them or high five them, they were making up a story that they are not important to you, they don't matter to you, or you don't care about them.

Then we wonder why our children, especially our teenagers, push us away. We wonder why we're so disconnected. We wonder why we have lost the ability to influence them or to advise them along their life's journey.

"Sawubona" is an African Zulu greeting and primal word that means, "I see you." It has a long history, and it means more than just the traditional hello.

If you were a member of the tribe, you would reply by saying, "Ngikhona," which means, "I am here," "I am here to be seen," or "I don't exist until I am recognized."

The order of the exchange is important. It means that until you see me, I do not exist, and when you see me, you bring me into existence.

The Zulu people believe that saying, "I am here to be seen" invokes the person's spirit to be present. "I am here" is a declaration of intent to fully inhabit this moment and fully engage.

If it's true that eyes are the windows to our soul, then when we make authentic eye contact with someone for long periods of time, our souls connect.

For whatever reason, when I make eye contact with someone for a longer period of time, my experience is we connect with each other on a deeper level.

Regardless of the words, I feel like we understand each other. I feel like I am you, you are me, and we are one.

When I connect with someone's eyes in a conversation, my listening becomes direct and sharp. It pulls me into the present moment, and all the background noise quiets down; all distractions seem to fade away.

Some of the benefits of being fully present and deeply connected with our children are that we:

- Validate who they are

- Confirm they matter to us

- Substantiate we love them

- Assure them we are here for them when they need us

- Affirm they can trust us

- Notice signs of distress when they don't reach out to us

- Appreciate things about them that we never noticed before

- Acknowledge them without necessarily needing words

I would hope one or two of these benefits are valuable enough for you to be committed to practicing the art of being more present in your life.

The starting point to becoming more present in the moment is to notice and observe all the distractions that are preventing you from naturally being present.

In today's world, not being present for most is automatic, like breathing. You have business to conduct, bills to pay, and kids to manage.

There is soccer practice at 5:00 p.m., dental appointments at 3:30 p.m., and elderly parents to look after.

However, with all of that and much more on your plate, and as daunting as it may seem to practice being present, I assure you it is possible.

Along with noticing all of the distractions you have in your life, another thing you need to be aware of is mind-wandering.

The overall mind-wandering rate for average Americans is 47% – meaning 47% of the time, people are thinking about other things than what they are currently doing.

When we mind-wander, we usually think about negative things with unpleasant outcomes.

One of my greatest gifts was during a 30-minute lecture when the lecturer painted a beautiful picture for me of the possibility that the past doesn't exist anymore and the future never comes.

The more I practice the art of being present, the more clarity I gain that the past really doesn't exist anymore. Now it becomes a waste of time to have worries or regrets about a particular time that isn't even relevant. If I can't change the past, then why would I entertain it?

Everything I can do about the past to either make it right or clean it up, or heal from it, all takes place now in the present moment.

Anytime I am thinking about past or future moments has me "mind-wandering," preventing me from being in the present moment.

One of the most harmful things I think we've learned as human beings is to multitask.

Multitasking in the right context can be a powerful tool to create results. Taken out of context and into your relationships, it can sabotage your efforts to be present and in the moment, connecting deeply with your family.

You cannot be effective when tending to two things at once, especially in relationships, and you have to decide if you want to be "here" or "there" in your head.

Women, you know what that's like? Try sharing your feelings and creating a deep, meaningful conversation with your husband or boyfriend while the football or basketball game is on TV within a fifteen-foot radius of him.

We can only do one thing at a time, so we ought to just focus on completing that one task wholeheartedly.

Being present is what we experience when we are completely at peace with this very moment. It is a life journey where we constantly grow our inner peace.

It may appear that being fully present in what we are doing at any one moment can be challenging because we have so many things vying for our attention. We are thinking about all the other things we have to do, want to do, or should be doing. A simple life has been replaced by a busy one.

When your mind is off daydreaming about something else you could be doing, you are not present. Your body might be here, but your mind and heart are somewhere else. It's impossible to make the kind of impact you want or fully experience something you enjoy if you aren't even here in the present moment.

Here is some contributing insight about *being* present from one of my good friends and a recognized thought leader in ontological, mindful, and ecological living: Bettie J. Spruill. Bettie is a world-renowned executive coach, management consultant, entrepreneur, and trainer with over 40 years of experience in the field of transformational leadership.

As toddlers, we learn to speak and to hear what others are saying, and we model the behaviors and actions of others. As we continue to grow and develop, we learn to read and write, along with other useful skills. However, few of us ever learn two of the most vital skills of all – being present and mindful.

Being present is a commitment to love. It takes practice to be present and to love. Being present is the gift of love and requires mindfulness. What is mindfulness?

Mindfulness, according to Jon Kabat-Zinn, the founder of mindfulness-based stress reduction (MBSR) is awareness, cultivated by paying attention in a sustained and particular way: on purpose, in the present moment, and nonjudgmentally.

Mindfulness is the practice of being present, to live in the here and now.

Mindfulness is deliberately paying full attention to what is occurring within you – in your body, heart, and mind – while also paying attention to what is happening around you. It's being aware of your moods, thoughts, and feelings, even your judgments and criticisms.

There once was a boy who always worried about what he would do with his life and how he would make a living. There simply wasn't time in his life to be happy. All he had time to do was plan for the future. He would tell himself, "I'll be happy once I get a career and start making money. Then I will be happy." He worked very hard indeed until he established himself in a good career where he was respected by many. But he wasn't happy. He was too busy thinking about all the things he didn't have. So he told himself, "I'll be happy once I have a family." And so it went on: He got married. He had kids. He had enough money to put them through school. He had grandkids and so on. However, there was always something. And in the end, he died, having had a wonderful life – yet he never took the time to appreciate it."

Being present happens in the present, not the past or the future. Being aware with real attention is a practice, and the more you practice, the better you get.

So learn to:

S – Stop

T – Take a breath

O – Observe your thinking and feelings – non-judgmentally

P – Proceed

This little process takes sustained practice. Mindfulness as a practice is available moment to moment. As you practice you will reap the rewards of this practice and so will your family. - Bettie Spruill

<hr>

Here are a few tips to help you practice being more present in your life.

1. Practice getting better each day in the ability to be a great observer. Observe more; think and talk less. As you practice this art form, you will start to see and feel things you couldn't see and feel before, allowing you to be more in the present moment. It's ok if your mind wanders a lot in the beginning. It's part of the awareness process. The more you practice, the better you will become.

2. Practice making eye contact with people. As you start to become more comfortable and confident making eye contact with others, you should start to notice you are not getting as distracted, allowing yourself to be more present and in the moment, connected to people and the conversation.

3. When you are in a conversation with your child, ask a lot of questions and practice listening intently to what they are saying. Practice hanging on each word. Surrender the urge to try to figure things out or coming up with solutions for them when they are talking. Silence the mind and just observe your child. Notice who they are choosing to be as they engage with you. Notice the words they choose or the faces they make, as they express themselves to you. Notice how you feel about them in the moment, and notice what they mean to you.

Here is an example. You are in a conversation with your son or daughter, and they start to share with you a moment when they were sad or confused. Instead of trying to figure out a solution for them or offer advice about how to handle the situation, I want you to observe the feeling you may be experiencing in that moment.

As they open up and reveal their sadness, I want you to give yourself permission to be open, honest, and vulnerable. Observe how you are feeling, and acknowledge your sadness for them. Keep asking open-ended questions. As the sharing ends, instead of trying to derive a solution for them or give them advice, ask them in a subtle way: What are you going to do? How are you going to handle it? What do you need from me to support you?" Then offer them a hug.

In closing I want to share with you from my opinion, one of the major interpersonal dysfunctions that most people have in common; is to desperately seek attention and approval from others.

Whether you are a child who needs it, or an adult who needs it, the constant need for other people's attention and approval is a horrible interpersonal disease. It's an addiction that makes people do abnormal things to get other people to give them the emotional pay-off that they yearn for.

Some payoffs include the need to get: attention, approval, sympathy, pity, sorrow, and to be right. No matter what the cost, what price they have to pay or what they have to give up or sacrifice to satisfy this empty void they feel within themselves. It is a very unhealthy behavior.

One of the ways to counter balance or detour this dysfunction from occurring for your children is to spend quality time with them in the present moment, giving them your undivided attention so that they get all of the emotional goodies that they need to be validated, as whole and complete.

I hope that I have helped you see a new perspective of the true value that your children can experience from you as a present and mindful parent; one that is critical for building emotionally centered and grounded human beings for our world.

DISTINCTION SIX
COMMITMENT

If you want to know about commitment, ask the mother who gets up two to three times a night to feed her newborn, goes to work for nine hours, drives home 30 miles in traffic, makes dinner for her family, does a few loads of wash, and repeats the process day after day.

When it comes to being rigorously committed to something or someone, your feelings don't matter anymore. What matters most is the promise you made to yourself or another that drives you to be and do whatever it takes to keep your promise.

Commitment is bigger than your feelings. Commitment is senior to all of your circumstances. It's greater than your excuses, superior to any and all justifications of why you can't.

"I don't feel like doing this today... So, what! Do it anyway." Committed people live by this creed.

Commitment is a relentless drive that we all possess; a powerful energy, a passion, and a purpose; a burning desire to complete something, to follow through with or to fulfill.

One of my favorite stories about commitment involves General George Washington. As he was approaching one of the fiercest war battles of his campaign, rumor has it that he and his troops had crossed over a bridge into battle when one of his officers came to him and asked whether he should burn the bridge behind them.

Burning the bridge behind you in the heat of battle was a statement to soldiers that there would be no retreating.

General Washington, contemplating his decision, looked onward toward the battlefield, back toward the bridge they had crossed, then back to the battlefield. Finally, he answered: "Burn the bridge; it's either victory or death."

This story reflects the stand I've taken in my own parenting commitment to my kids, relentlessly dedicated to them winning big in their lives. When I think about my commitment to my children, I think about a promise I made to them when they were born.

I held each one of them in my arms after their birth. As I fed each one of them their bottle, I remember the powerful connection we made with each other, as we both locked eyes, falling deeper and deeper in love with one another. I remember vividly the vow I made to each child:

"I love you with all my heart, and I am grateful and honored to be your dad. I promise to always love you, to always look after you, to always do my best to teach you all the things you need to learn, to live an amazing life. I

pledge my life to never give up on you and always fight for your greatness."

So, when they talk back to me, roll their eyes at me, try and push me away, and even ignore me, I always remember the commitment I made to them when we locked eyes and fell deeply in love with each other.

Quite often, I see the frustration in parents because the relationship with their children is strained. I often wonder if they've forgotten the promise they made to their babies, to never give up and always fight for their greatness.

I know you haven't given up on your kids because you are still reading this book. It says a lot about your commitment to your kids and to the relationship you want to keep building upon.

When I was exploring my options on how to write this book, I asked some of my colleagues, friends, and fellow coaches to contribute. I knew this book was going to be something special.

I asked one of my good friends and greatest teachers of all time to share with you his views on commitment. Dr. Ray Blanchard is a master trainer, seminar designer, corporate consultant, and a true lifestyle architect.

Ray has influenced the lives of more than 200,000 individuals all over the world as a master trainer and consultant. He will undoubtedly make an impact on millions more from his contribution through this book:

THE TRANSFORMATIVE POWER IN ACTION

Dr. Ray Blanchard

Commitment is the energetic force that transforms possibility into predictability.

There are those people who seem to always be focused and headed in a positive direction, and who seem to be getting things done. Then there are those who talk about achievement but never seem to get it together or never seem to have things materialize. Commitment is the difference – It separates doers from dreamers.

Commitment is engaging; it has charge and aliveness. People tend to notice the electricity it generates. It also has direction and intent toward a destination or end result. People do not follow uncommitted leaders who ramble and waste energy. They tend to follow those who possess charisma defined by their commitment that has direction, aliveness, and charge.

Most often, commitment goes with action. More than the subjective conviction, the critical point is commitment involves focused and persistent action. Action without commitment is merely a motion. Action with commitment can change your world.

It is often displayed in your work habits by the hours you keep. Sometimes it is seen by your willingness to go beyond the pale or putting yourself on the line to do whatever it takes to get the job done. In other quarters, it might be displayed by the diligence you demonstrate to continuously improve yourself or your abilities. Yes, in relationships, it can be witnessed by the will to stand in the tough times and see things through to the other side.

Overall, commitment is a vigilant dedication to a cause that lifts you to extraordinary performance to get your intended result. It is the steady force that helps you keep your vows, pledges, obligations, and promises.

1. **It Comes from The Heart**. Many people want guaranteed outcomes before they put their all into something. They want to know the score of the game before they play. They stick their toe in the water, without being fully engaged. They are cautious and concerned with what negatives will happen rather than with their passions and the rewards. They focus on how others will react. They play not to lose. They are usually followers and not the leaders, the wannabes and not the celebrities, the losers and not the winners. However, commitment precedes outstanding achievement. It is the steadfast desire that starts from the fire in the heart – the fuel that drives the machine! Until there is a commitment, there may be no purpose to act at all, let alone achieve greatness. Viktor Frankl, Michael Jordan, and Serena Williams are generational examples of such fuel and fire. Long distance runners are often spoken

about in this light because they keep going after they hit the wall. Their no-quit attitude and a driving force of pure intention helped them to transcend their discomforts and, to some extent, intense pain.I am told that in the Kentucky Derby, the winning horse effectively runs out of oxygen after the first half mile, and it goes the rest of the way on heart.

2. **It Is Revealed in Action**. It is one thing to talk about commitment. It is another to live it day to day. As usual, it is easier to do the talk than to do the walk. At the end of the day, commitment is revealed by the choices you make at critical crossroads, as well as the action you take to move forward.

3. **Commitment is Not Always Safe**. As John F. Kennedy said, "There are risks and costs to action. But they are far less than the long-range costs of comfortable inaction." Inaction is often the consequence of overindulging in strategies for safety.

4. **Overthinking and Overanalyzing** These often eclipse achievement because commitment to the positive result is missing. Instead, too much time is spent being too reasonable, trying to figure out how not to fail or look bad, how not to risk too much, or how to be safe and in control. This leads to imagined obstacles and difficulties that may not be present, which gets you off track. In the

end, you lose what you really want rather than taking committed action to achieve it.

5. **It is Measured by Follow Through**. The demonstration of commitment is in establishing your priorities and following through on them. Anyone who acts only when he or she is in the mood or when it's convenient is not going to be successful. They will neither gain respect nor be able to be a positive influence on others. Extended commitment takes discipline. After identifying your heartfelt commitments, you need a structure for fulfillment. It is necessary to make a discrete plan, a roadmap. It keeps you from wasting precious time. If you can determine what's really a priority and make a map to follow, it releases you from the "everything else" of life. It is freedom with direction, and it's a lot easier to follow through on what's important. That is the essence of disciplined commitment in action.

6. **It Builds Confidence and Reduces Stress**. Too many people think their freedom comes from operating without a plan and having the liberty to be autonomous and without restrictions. However, having structure allows you to develop agility and flexibility within guidelines. You can make adjustments while still engaged in the process of moving forward with direction. This can be very powerful. Without this navigation tool,

the risk is to become scattered, like an octopus on roller blades – disastrous!

7. **Disciplined Commitment** Most successful people who are in control of their destiny realize disciplined commitment based on real priorities is critical. However, it is not a one-time affair; it must be repetitive until it becomes a practice, a lifestyle. Therefore, embrace your truth, and then develop systems and routines, especially in the areas crucial to your long-term growth and success. This increases your confidence, reduces your stress, and allows you the ability to relax in the face of challenge. You build more trust in yourself to emotionally and behaviorally respond to life more appropriately.

8. **It Is the Gateway to Accomplishment**. Through all endeavors and relationships, we face obstacles and challenges. There have been people with extreme hardships and high hopes or dreams, and commitment was the only thing that carried them forward.
    It has been said by high achievers: If you are knocked down seven times, get up eight. That is the way of the committed warrior, fortified with the serious promise to press on, to get back up, no matter how many setbacks you have. It is this kind of conviction that gives rise to divine providence, which is working in your favor by showing you possibilities and opportunities you may

not have seen without having been committed. Where does this commitment come from? It comes from having things matter to you in a heartfelt way, your true yearnings, or being obedient to a powerful calling that is beyond your personal affections and desires.

How to Elevate Your Commitment

Be Deliberate: Sometimes we think we are committed to something, but our actions say otherwise. In checking your calendar, your belongings, your checkbook, or time with family, evaluate how you are spending your time and money. All these indicate where you are committed and may suggest places where you might want to make some deliberate adjustments.

Know Your Truth (What is Worthy of Your Life): One of the most relevant questions we get to ask ourselves is what really matters to us. When it comes down to it, what in life is worth giving your life for? What would you not be able to *be*, *do*, or *have*? What would you simply not do without, or not stop doing, no matter what? Are you living consistently with your answers? Shift your commitments and actions to what really matters to you.

Put Both Feet In: Commitment is complete. You may be saying you are committed to several things, but in each case, the commitment may or may not be there completely. Most successful people say 99% commitment is the same as zero. If you were going to jump over the Snake River Canyon, you need to jump 100%, or you are flat on your butt. It is all or nothing – pregnant or not, as they say. So commit 100%.

Go Public: When you have an idea you are hot on, go tell the world. Then go into your workshop or studio and invent it. By making your ideas and plans more public, you add more expectations for you to follow through more rigorously.

It is your job, and only yours, to identify a purpose or vision that is worth your life and giving your heart and soul to. Then follow through. When you do, your life will be new, adventurous, and thoroughly transformed. In The Open Door, the blind, deaf, author, Helen Keller, said it clearly: "Life is either a daring adventure or nothing at all."

— ◆ —

Wow! Ray lands some very powerful points for me, helping me examine my next level of commitment when it comes to parenting and my life.

As I take a more committed stand for myself, I become a more powerful leader. I deliver on my promises. I keep my word, and I push myself beyond the walls and limits of the status quo. Then I realize the positive effects it has on my little ones. They are always watching and observing so intently, searching for reasons to look up to me.

My experience and truth are reflected in Dr. Blanchard's statement: *"People don't follow uncommitted leaders who ramble and waste energy; they follow those who possess the charisma defined by commitment."*

All people, including our own kids, follow someone. Your kids want to be led, and they want to follow someone who inspires them and empowers them to rise to a higher level of greatness. They will follow the lead of the people they admire and trust the most, those they have deemed worthy enough to be followed. Why not decide to be that kind of leader?

When my son was in high school, he was a great football player. Depending on his senior performance, a few colleges had him on their radar, with potential scholarship offers on the table. One Friday night under the lights, a few games into the season, he broke his leg in two places, needing two metal screws to put his leg back together. In an instant, his dream to help his team win a championship was shattered. My son was devastated and thought he would never play football again.

On one of his depressing days, as he sat on the couch feeling sorry for himself, I told him not only was he going to play football again, but also, he was going to play football at the college level.

I told him I was not going to give up on him, and I was fully committed to getting him back on that field if that's what he wanted, no matter what it took.

Somehow, he believed me. Every day at 2 p.m., I put him and his wheelchair in our Dodge Durango, and we drove to the football field where his team practiced. I rolled him in his wheelchair and positioned him at the end zone and threw 200-400 footballs at him every day for the rest of the season.

My son not only developed better eye-hand coordination, but he also developed a greater self-esteem and an extraordinary level of confidence. He learned what true commitment was all about. And the following year, as a freshman at Moorpark College, he led his team in receiving yards and touchdowns as one of their starting receivers. I can only hope, one day, he will remember one of many committed stands I took for him and make that same or even greater commitment to his kids.

Dr. Ray so eloquently stated, *"Commitment is the steadfast desire that starts from the heart. It is the fuel that drives the machine."*

That desire from the heart and the fuel that drives the machine is your love. It is the huge amount of endless love you have for your kids, the unselfishness in you that wants them to win big in their life, which far exceeds all of your own accomplishments, your own dreams, joys and experiences in your life.

Isn't that what all parents want for their kids? To help them live a more abundant and prosperous life than we did? We pass the torch on to our kids, leaving behind a legacy that we can truly be proud of.

When Dr. Ray says commitment comes from *"having things matter to you in a heartfelt way, your true yearnings, or being obedient to a powerful calling that is beyond your personal affections and desires,"* it brings me back to the commitment I made to my newborn babies. When I made that commitment to them, I made it from a place deep inside my soul, a place where I knew being their father was my deep calling.

When you realize what a great honor it is to be mom or dad to your kids and fully embrace it as your calling or higher purpose, I believe you will reconnect to what matters most to you, and to them.

You will start to focus on what is most important, and let go of the things that really don't matter as much. You will be freed up to re-invent your new commitment to parenting.

To wrap up Dr. Ray's wisdom on this distinction on commitment, I will use one of his perennial statements: *"Committed people are influential. They inspire others because of where they are willing to go to overcome and win."*

This one statement says it all for me, partly because I hear the cries of thousands of teenagers.

What they all seem to have in common in their heartbreak is feeling like their parents have given up on them, to some degree. They believe their parents are no longer committed to them winning in life as they once were, noticing their parents have resigned to a certain level of hopelessness and despair, settling for the status quo.

They can see that their parents, through their own frustrations and disappointments, no longer operate from "playing to win," but have resigned to "playing not to lose."

What teens say about parents who are "playing not to lose:"

- My parents do just enough to get by – no more, no less

- They're pessimistic – always prepared for worst case scenarios

- They worry about what might go wrong, instead of trusting in what will go right

- They stick to the old ways of doing things – unwilling to change

- They get worried and anxious when things don't go as planned

- When I push them away, they give up – not realizing I am just scared

- They no longer believe in me and what I may be capable of creating

- They take things personally and make it about them when it's not

- They're not open to other possibilities – fixed in their points of view

- They hang out too long in the problem – they don't seek new solutions

- They don't trust me but then wonder why I don't trust them

I want to share a story with you about a woman named Grace, who reached out to me to help her 16-year-old son, Christian.

I agreed to meet with her first one-on-one to get a better understanding of how exactly she wanted me to help her son. During that hour-long meeting, she cried in my office, sharing with me the pain and heartbreak that she struggles with daily, watching her son Christian slowly exclude himself from his family, hiding out in his room, disconnecting, and pushing away the very people who love him the most.

Grace described all she had tried to do to motivate Christian to open up, to engage, to be that loving and carefree boy that she once knew him to be. She was overwhelmed by all the failed attempts to make any difference.

I asked her to share with me a little bit about the home she has provided for Christian (like details about her family such as who lived in their home and the general environment of their home).

She painted a gray picture of her relationship with her husband, Christian's' father, and their younger son, Tommy. Although Grace and her husband both live in the home, their marriage had been on the rocks for the past few years. After getting Grace to share with me and paint a clearer picture of what Christian might be experiencing in his home, I explained to her that Christian's behavior was a symptom of, or a direct reflection of, the kind of energy or states of being manifested in their home – for children live what they learn and learn what they live.

I asked Grace to describe her and her husband's ways of being in the home since their marriage and relationship had hit a low point. After 45 minutes of getting her to take a deep conscientious look at this question, and through some encouragement and compassion on my part, Grace was finally able to make an honest assessment. Her list included disappointment, hopelessness, insecurity, embarrassment, and disconnection.

I asked her if she thought this kind of energy in the home could possibly be an underlying source or root cause of Christian's symptoms. After she had begun to cry, she answered: "Yes, I do." I informed her I could not help her son directly, but indirectly I could. I told her, if she wanted to help save him from despair, it would ultimately be up to her. I told her that it was going to take an extraordinary level of commitment, unlike anything she has ever dedicated herself to before. I asked her if she was up for the task. After a little hesitation, she ultimately said, "Yes."

I asked her to write down on her trusty notepad these words: "If it's to *be*, it's up to me." Right there in a new moment of clarity, Grace created an affirmation that would ultimately and undeniably help her to cause a shift in her son, giving her the loving, playful and engaged little boy she was so desperately seeking. I told her if she wanted this game plan to work, she needed to *be* 100% coachable, and 100% committed. She wholeheartedly agreed.

We began to work on her relationship with her husband to cause the kind of shift in the home Christian needed. After she was done giving me all the excuses why it hasn't worked in the past, our coaching got her past some of the resentment she was holding.

Ending our first session with some powerful breakthroughs, Grace returned the following week with her husband. After a powerful session with Grace and her husband, and some homework for both of them, I received a grateful text message from Grace a few weeks later, thanking me for my help.

After a few more sessions, Grace opened up and shared both Christian and Tommy have both emphatically responded to the shift in their home. She enthusiastically said, "Christian is now coming out of his room and freely joining in on family discussions, family dinners, and even partaking in family outings. I'm so grateful; this is exactly what I've wanted for him and for us."

She said, after this experience, she realized she had been too controlling toward Christian, trying to force him, making him feel guilty, and even punishing him if he didn't show up the way she wanted him to. She understood it took this experience and this kind of awareness to be rigorously committed to producing these profound outcomes.

I acknowledged them both for their efforts to put commitment back into their relationship, and ultimately, a new commitment to their son's well-being. They were asked to distinctly identify the *ways of being* that had shifted in them individually, in their relationship, and in their home. Her list included: Happy, Hopeful, Connected, Forgiving, Trusting, Vulnerable, Loving, and Committed.

Her husband's list included: Responsible, Open, Inviting, Connected, Forgiving, Fun, and Committed.

I asked them to title their list "The Magical Ingredients for Effective Parenting," as a reminder to remember they always and already have everything they need to *be* extraordinary parents. They now know they can create the kind of results they are committed to creating in their family life, and it's never too late to make a new commitment.

Some of the most inspiring stories I've heard come from parents who are courageous enough to finally be honest with their kids – owning up to their own shortcomings as a parent, willing to ask their kids to have patience while they learn how to be better parents. That's inspirational!

Children absolutely love to hear this kind of authentic communication from parents, with real admissions, including sincere requests for patience. It shows a true commitment to reach your full parenting potential.

Here are a few suggestions to help you practice the art of commitment:

1. Start with something small to dedicate yourself to

2. Decide it's going to happen no matter what

3. Stay consistent with your efforts until you complete the task

4. Repeat this process until it becomes a habit

Declare your commitment aloud in the presence of others, so you are more likely to be accountable. Also, put something at stake if you don't follow through. For example, make an agreement with someone that, if you don't follow through with your commitment, you will buy them an expensive lunch or dinner or you will donate something of great value to a non-profit.

Get yourself an accountability buddy, coach, or mentor to keep you on track and hold you accountable. Identify and eliminate the distractions in your life that keep you from fulfilling your commitments. Forgive yourself for not following through with your broken commitments. Ask for forgiveness from those you have broken your commitments to, and ask how they would want you to repair it. Then recommit with a new and greater intention.

There is nothing more inspiring than the unwavering and relentless commitment of a mother or father to help their child become a powerful, heartfelt, and self-directed leader. It is the way of the committed parent to keep fighting for their kids to ultimately succeed in life, with a mighty purpose, a deep burning passion, and as much joy and freedom that their hearts can handle.

I believe you are that parent! Your kids are lucky to have such a true warrior – a parent as courageously loving and committed as you.

DISTINCTION SEVEN
RESPONSIBILITY

Being responsible is about taking 100% accountability for your life and the manner in which it unfolds.

It is living your life and choosing to take 100% responsibility for your thoughts, feelings, choices, and actions. It involves stepping up and owning your life, as well as how you may have contributed to your results.

It is admitting to yourself that you play a part in it all, regardless of the circumstances that seem like you don't.

There's something to be said about people who live their life by this principle called responsibility.

People who choose to take responsibility for their life are often seen as powerful people, well respected and admired.

Why?

It's far too easy to blame others for any and all circumstances that may occur in one's life. It's easy to pass the buck, point fingers, or find excuses to not own up to the part you've played in the matter, whether it was directly or indirectly.

In society, we have slowly been conditioned to blame external factors as the fault or the reasons why we face what we don't like.

It could be as simple as blaming your brother or sister when you were young, or blaming your mom or dad for the reasons why your life is the way it is, and before you know it, you have unconsciously trained yourself to condemn and/or accuse someone else for the way that your life turned out.

Anyone can blame; however, not everyone can rise to a higher standard and be accountable for how they may have contributed to their results.

Responsibility has many layers to it. There are the things I know I am responsible for. There are things I don't know I am responsible for. There are things I know that I don't know I am responsible for. And there are things I don't know that I don't know I am responsible for.

I know it sounds like double-talk, but it's not. It's the process of awakening to a new possibility that there are many layers of growth.

Things I know I am responsible for:

My life, well-being, growth, thoughts, feelings, choices, and actions.

Things I don't know I am responsible for:

All the things I can choose to be responsible for but don't because, from my current point of view, I can only see that I am not responsible for them.

Things I know that I don't know I am responsible for:

All the things I ignore or live in the illusion that I'm not responsible for. If someone, who I trusted, respected and valued pointed them out to me, I would acknowledge that I am responsible for them.

Things I don't know that I don't know I am responsible for:

Everything else.

Some of you will understand that example, and some of you won't – and that's ok. I will look at how I can give you easier examples or more compelling stories that could open up that possibility for you.

Let me tell you why it's important to learn how to take responsibility for more of your life on a broader scale and a deeper level.

When you choose to take responsibility for all of the circumstances and state of affairs in your life, it directly puts you at the center of your universe.

You will be living your life as the source. You are the owner; you're at the cause, authoring your choices and manifesting your results.

It puts you directly in the driver's seat of your life, giving you conscious control of the wheel.

If you relinquish the option to take 100% responsibility for your life, it leaves room for you to choose the victim perspective, where you are not in control, where it appears to you that there is nothing you can do about it.

The victim perspective renders you powerless to change any outcome and gives you a platform to constantly blame others for your life not turning out the way you intended.

This is one of the powerful perspective shifts I have discovered and learned through rigorous Transformational Leadership Training.

Whether consciously or unconsciously, you are always choosing either the responsibility or victim lenses, through which you see the world.

Imagine wearing a pair of invisible glasses with one lens that allows you to see the responsible perspective of your life, and the other lens allows you to see the victim perspective.

How do you think those lenses affect your point of view?

How do you think those lenses affect your choices?

How would those points of view and choices affect the way others see you in their lives?

Would they respect and admire you? Would they tolerate and disdain you?

From my experience, the people who choose to live their lives from the victim perspective are not always well received as a leader, mentor, or confidant; others don't turn to them for advice or seek their opinions for inspiration and empowerment.

Why?

They are easily perceived as weak, powerless, incapable, whiny, and wimpy – as the complainer.

Ultimately, these types of leaders appear to be disempowering and a turn-off. They are not appealing by any means; they are repelling.

Quite often, "turning off" is one of the underlying reasons why teenagers stop listening to their parents.

Parents who are constantly pointing fingers at them – making them bad and wrong for choices they may not yet have the capacity to understand – simply cannot inspire their kids.

On the other hand, if you are constantly choosing to take full responsibility for your thoughts, feelings, choices, and actions, you appear to teenagers as the kind of person who they can trust.

Responsible leaders appear to be safe and trustworthy.

In a world where most people are quick to blame and fault others, responsible leaders are a rare and unique breed. They are the kind of people others turn to, feeling safe enough to open up and share, revealing more of themselves.

Don't you want to *be* that person for your child/children?

So, here is why it's important to start living your life by *being* more responsible:

- People respect you – you gain their trust

- You earn a higher level of credibility with people

- You model and teach others how to take responsibility for their lives

- People feel safe around you, compelled to admit their mistakes and reach out

- You become the kind of person who people admire

- You become more confident in your ability to solve the problem or find the solution

- People in your life enjoy being a part of your team, willing to align with you

- You win people over and hook their hearts

- You make more effective decisions

- People feel inspired by your honesty and bravery

- You become more in control of your relationships

- You don't have to be in any more arguments about who is right

Let me share a story with you about a friend who called and asked me to help him with his 16-year-old daughter.

My friend was frustrated with his daughter and called me for some advice.

I met my friend one Saturday morning at Starbucks and asked what was going on.

He spent the next 45 minutes on a victim rant describing how his daughter doesn't listen to him, respect him, or do anything she is told to do.

After 45 minutes, I stopped him and said: "I have a 45-minute rule.

He looked at me weird and asked, "What's the rule?"

"I can only sit here – being a loving and compassionate space for you, while you choose to be the victim in your story – for 45 minutes. After that I cannot let you continue," I said.

My friend chuckled and looked at me very confused and said, "I don't understand."

"Whenever I meet with a client or help a parent for the first time, I only let them be the victim in their story for up to 45 minutes, and that is the maximum," I said.

I explained to him the two life perspectives called victim/responsible. After about 20 minutes of explaining this mindset, my friend sat back for a brief moment and started to tear up.

As I do in all of my sessions, I asked him the magic question, "What are you hearing me say?"

He looked at me with a somber face, tears running down his cheeks and said:

"What I hear you say, Alex, is I have been blaming her all this time, making it her fault that she is rude, disrespectful, and non-compliant. I never realized until now that I had played a part in her world, in her environment, which has caused her to behave like that. This whole time I have been living in a falsehood that she just all of a sudden woke up one day and decided to behave like this on her own, without me having any part to play in the matter. I now can see, and it hurts. But it's a good hurt – this is my wake-up call. I am ultimately responsible for the way my daughter has slowly been showing up to me in our relationship; I just never saw it so clearly before."

I acknowledged my friend for his courage and willingness to dig deep and take an honest look at his parenting, to see how he could take responsibility for his daughter's behaviors.

I asked him if he could recall any choices or behaviors that could have caused her to be so angry, hurt, resentful, discouraged, or betrayed.

My friend looked down for a moment cried some more before regaining his composure. He looked back at me and said, *"Yes, I can. I have been short with her many times, not giving her the time she needs when she comes to me wanting to share.*

I have been really controlling when it comes to her wanting to go hang out with her friends because of my own fears. I haven't been as open minded as I could have been with some of her ideas and suggestions of how she wants to start living her own life.

Yeah, I guess there are a lot of things I have to go back and look at regarding the way I parent and the way I might be showing up to her, from her perspective, that is causing these current behavioral issues.

I think the biggest wake-up call I had this morning is realizing I've been choosing the victim perspective, as though she is doing all of this to me, rather than choosing the responsible perspective and seeing how I could have caused, created, or at the very least, co-created these results.

From victim mode, I cannot change any of it. I can only gripe, moan, complain, and look for other people to fix it for me.

Being willing to look at the responsible version of my parenting and how she could be experiencing me gives me the power to make the necessary changes or adjustments that she needs from me to feel loved, supported, and uplifted in her life – rather than feeling trapped, not heard, or invalidated as the beautiful and powerful young lady I want her to be."

As I sit here reliving this moment, it brings warmth to my heart knowing that, because of his courageous and bold effort to really dig deep and be completely honest with himself, he experienced a profound awakening, a new awareness of how he was getting in the way of his daughter winning in life.

I have many successful parenting stories, but they don't all turn out like this.

As much as I have seen the brave and honest parent willing to really look deep to find a way to *be* responsible for the results of their relationship with their teenagers, I also have had many who are not willing to.

When I share this gift of perspective shifting with parents, some parents, for whatever reason, don't get it, don't want to get it, refuse to get it, don't believe in it, can't see the value of it, or simply don't want to go down that road.

Why?

I believe it's much easier for them to ignore, complain, tolerate, justify, blame, or seek other professionals to try to change their child for them.

Another possibility is they could be addicted to the drama, unaware of the interpersonal addiction to the payoff they get from being the victim.

As a payoff, we get attention, pity, sorrow, and sympathy from others. We get to be right, to avoid, to be validated that it's not our fault. We also get an excuse to not take accountability for the result, or do something different about it.

For those of you who are starting to get it, let's move on to a few examples to help you see if you can gain a better understanding of the value of taking 100% responsibility for your relationships.

Victim: It's happening to me. I can't change it. My hands are tied. I am powerless.

My son will not take out the trash. He is so lazy, not motivated to help out around the house one bit. I have to always remind him, staying on top of him constantly to take the trash out and do his chores; I can't believe he is so selfish. He only does things that benefit him and what he needs to do for himself.

He would rather play video games or make himself busy doing non-productive stuff than the chores we have given him. It's as if he doesn't take any accountability for anything around here. He's only showing me he is not a responsible person. How can I trust him when he doesn't do the things we have asked of him?

I don't know what else to do; I can't get him to want to help out around here. Is there anything you can say to him to get him to understand that he needs to take the trash out twice a day without me constantly nagging him?"

In the above narrative, the parent looks through a perspective filter that convinces him/her that their teen has a behavioral flaw that has nothing to do with them.

The parent is acting as if there is nothing he/she did or didn't do that contributed to his current behaviors. In this mindset, the parent has rendered themselves powerless and cannot change the result because he/she lives in the illusion their son is the only one that can change it.

Here is the crazy part of this scenario: If I would sit down with the son and ask him why he isn't doing his chores or helping out around the house by taking the trash out, I almost guarantee he would give me the same victim version about his mom or dad. It would sound almost similar to the one you just read from the parent.

Responsible: I played a part in this. I can change it if I change myself.

The reason why my son won't take the trash out when I ask him to is that, to some degree, I have conditioned him to believe he doesn't have to do anything when he doesn't feel like it.

I have made his life easy for him to not have any urgency. I obviously have not taught him how to live his life willfully with intention and purpose. I have not created value big enough for him to see how important it is to follow through with his commitments, agreements, or promises.

I need to teach him what an honor it is to be in contribution and to be a team player, doing his part to keep this family running smoothly.

Based on results, there are a lot of things I still need to teach him that I obviously never did. I have to learn how to find new ways to model and teach what I want him to learn. I have to give up thinking that, just because I taught him once or twice, he actually learned it."

The parent in the above narrative has realized that, through their ability to be open-minded, they absolutely have played a part in the dysfunctions and behavioral patterns in their teen. The responsible perspective filter helps the parent realize that they need to course correct themselves.

This perspective has the parent operating from being proactive, not reactive. Proactive-ness is born out of your willingness to take responsibility for the outcome. From the responsible perspective shift, this parent can see that, if they make the necessary changes in their parenting, the results will change.

One of the biggest universal secrets to parenting is our children's dysfunctions are merely a byproduct of our own parenting. They are a symptom of an underlying issue we, as the parent, need to improve on in our own inner abilities.

Our children respond to who we are being and who we are not being. When we are vulnerable and let them in, they become vulnerable and let us in. When we are fearful and controlling, they become fearful and controlling.

Ultimately, if we are loving, patient, compassionate, playful, and trusting, our kids respond beautifully.

Just a few minor shortcomings in our inability to *be* what they need from us can totally tweak the results, depending on how much more work we need to complete.

As you can see, the areas in which we might need to improve will be reflected in the way our kids show up in our lives, the way they show up in our relationships, as well as in their behaviors and the manner in which they interact with us.

Some of us just need to put a more conscious effort in certain areas of improvement. Some of us are naturally more effective in some areas, and some of us lack growth in other areas.

Then there are some of us who won't even admit there are any areas of improvement left for us to attain.

Those people will look for evidence to validate they are being and doing everything right as a parent, so it must be their child's fault that their sadness, depression, behavioral issues, and addictions are brought on by their own doing. I will assume that you purchased this book because you are open minded, that you realize learning never stops, and there is so much more growth to be completed as a parent so that you can keep fighting for your kids to keep accessing their full potential.

With that in mind, I will talk to you as though you are starting to understand how critical it is to take responsibility not only for your life but for the results you have authored or co-authored with your child or children.

I am going to share with you some of my "a-ha moments" where I took responsibility for my results along my parenting journey.

Scenario #1:

One of my kids would often take their frustration out on their mother, but not with me.

Responsible Perspective:

"I must have at some point in my marriage taken my own frustration out on my wife in front of my kids, for one of them to think it's OK to do that. I obviously wasn't modeling respect for my wife's points of views even if they differed from mine."

Adjustment:

I need to manage my emotions in a healthy way, be more patient with my wife, more compassionate, more forgiving, being respectful of her points of views and honor the way she chooses to share, especially in front of my kids.

Scenario #2:

One of my teens was heartbroken and snuck out of the house in the middle of the night and took my car. I woke up from a sound I heard in my driveway and saw my car missing, so I called the police, and they found my car. I got my car and my teenager back.

Responsible Perspective:

I am obviously not as connected to my teen as I thought I was, unaware they are going through difficulties in their life, not being vulnerable, compassionate, present and inviting enough for them to let me in; so I can help them manage their frustrations and stressors.

Adjustment:

I need to be more present, attentive, and available to them. I need to be more playful and lighthearted and share myself more to gain their trust.

Scenario #3:

One of my kids quite often would doubt herself and worry a lot about not knowing her purpose in life. She looked sad, depressed, and at times, seemed frustrated with the unknown.

Responsible Perspective:

Perhaps if I spent more quality time with my teen and kept reminding them how special they are and the gifts I see in them, they would be excited, inspired, and eager to follow their passions and chase their dreams.

Adjustment:

I need to be more encouraging, validating their existence. I need to keep speaking into their greatness and keep reminding them they are special and have a huge gift to offer the world. I need to spend more quality time helping them discover for themselves their likes, their wants, their desires.

Learning how to *be* responsible in my life is one of the greatest gifts I could have ever given myself.

I use it everywhere I go, with every relationship I have, and every scenario I am in.

Does it mean every relationship I have is perfect? Absolutely, not.

Many components of relationships and things are out of my control. I cannot and will not ever be able to make them perfect, but taking responsibility for them rather than being the victim is more powerful, much more freeing, and more effective in the relationships that matter most.

Taking responsibility is not blaming yourself.

Blame is unhealthy and emotionally damaging. It sabotages our efforts and keeps us stuck, unable to move forward freely and powerfully.

Being responsible is a position you take, like a platform to stand on. It's a principle you decide to live your life by, a higher standard that guides you to never give up your power.

Taking responsibility is more like an honor to model your life to others. It's a statement you make to the world, pledging that people can feel safe around you because you won't ever make them feel alone – like they're carrying the burden and weight all by themselves.

The last thing I want to say about responsibility is it has magical powers. Don't ask me how because I don't know how it works, but I will explain the magic to give you an idea of its power.

The energy derived from responsibility is contagious, and that's what I teach!

Here is a recent scenario:

One of my clients is a prominent leader in our community.

During one of my sessions, he asked me a question about helping one of his employees.

The question was: *"Alex how do I get one of my employees to start taking responsibility for some of the errors they keep making and the constant mistakes that keep happening on their end?"*

I replied, *"Oh, I have a secret formula for that. Do you want to know what it is?"*

"Yes… tell me what it is," he said.

"I will only reveal it to you if you promise to go practice it right now," I said.

"Absolutely, I will," he said.

My instructions to my client were to walk over to his employee and get permission to have a "clean-up" conversation with him/her. The clean-up conversation was going to start with my client first apologizing to his employee, for whatever mistake or error that was made.

Then, I asked my client to "own up" and take responsibility for the mishap, finding an authentic reason how they could have played a part in the error and revealing their finding to that employee.

After I had finished instructing my client, he looked at me and said, *"Ok, then what?"*

"Then watch your employee interrupt you at a certain point to start taking responsibility for the mistake he/she made," I said.

"No… it can't be that easy," he said.

So, I bet him a dollar.

We both shook hands to seal the bet, and we walked over to the employee. I hid around the corner and listened to the conversation, and guess what? I won a dollar.

My client met me back in his office and was stunned at the results. He asked me: *"How did that happen?"*

It seems to be this weird phenomenon: What you model and project into a conversation or relationship, you get back. In essence, you mirror to the other person that which seems logical and the right thing to do, and they just serve it back to you.

I advised my client to practice taking responsibility in every scenario where something didn't go right, or the way it was planned, or the way they wanted it to look.

Then watch the other person, right in front of your eyes, reciprocate the honor of owning up to their part.

In one experiment, I saw two people argue about who is responsible for the mishap. It was quite amusing and, yet, so amazing at the same time.

Now, be prepared that some people have a longer learning curve than others do. Most teens may need to see the example repeatedly until the phenomenon finally transpires.

Don't give up. I promise that, in time, you will eventually teach your kids what it looks like to be responsible, and soon you will be shocked as they start to be and do the same.

Parent Training Tip:

Practicing the art of being compassionate toward your kids helps free you up more to accept responsibility for the relationship at a higher level.

The compassion comes from realizing that your son or daughter is doing the best they can with what tools you have given them through your teaching and modeling.

Remember they are still young. Their brain hasn't fully developed – and if they have experienced any dysfunctions at the home, like yelling, divorce, loss, spoiling, enabling, coddling, not being heard, not being validated, or not being seen – they might need a mom or dad that has more patience, understanding, and tolerance to give.

I invite you to find it in your heart to *be* compassionate enough toward your kids, allowing you to take the high road and show them what responsibility looks like.

Below are a few suggestions on how to take responsibility:

1. Start a responsibility journal. Write down all the things that happen to you in a day or a week, and practice writing out two or three new ways to perceive yourself playing a part in the result. How did you contribute in some way? The more creative you get, the better you become.

2. Whenever you find yourself blaming others or choosing the victim perspective, find someone you trust, and instead of whining, complaining, or blaming in your rant to them, share with them a version where ultimately you are contributing to the scenario. Own up to it!

3. Pay attention to how you deal with situations. Be fully aware of the stories you make up surrounding an event or a situation, and then evaluate it. Look to see if you are blaming anyone, faulting them, accusing them, or criticizing their choices. The more you notice it and become conscious of the process and the habit you have

created, the more likely you will realize you can change it.

DISTINCTION EIGHT
INSPIRATIONAL

When I was a young man, I had a handful of people who really inspired me in my life, who truly took a stand for me. There was surely something different about them. They definitely stood out from all of the other people who simply wanted the best for me.

Every individual who has inspired me throughout my life had tremendous faith and belief in my abilities, far beyond my own capacity.

Every one of them had an uncommon vision of me, a unique perception. They saw me in a particular way I could not yet see for myself. It was like they were looking at me through a certain set of lenses that saw no wrong. I call those lenses 'The Greatness Glasses.'

All those who inspired me wore such glasses and were able to recognize my greatness when I couldn't. They were able to identify certain qualities and gifts within me, despite all of my own evidence indicating I was average and ordinary; they saw differently.

They didn't care about my past, my faults, my failures, or my shortcomings; they only cared about my capabilities, and they directly focused only on my potential.

Also, they all seemed to have this amazing ability to speak into that potential greatness with a passion and fervor.

Here are some of those examples:

"Alex, you are not going to quit! Over my dead body. You know why? Because you are not a quitter. You, my friend, are a warrior. Warriors don't quit. They feel their fear and take it into battle with them. There's no one more qualified than you to take on this challenge, and to be honest with you, you're the only one I would trust to take it on anyway. So, stop wasting my time with this quitting nonsense, and let's go!"

"Alex, I want you to know that you're amazing! I know sometimes you're challenged at seeing that within yourself, but I wish you could see yourself with my eyes. If you could, you would see nothing but a courageous leader, with a big heart – one that cares for people and one that makes people feel safe and heard. You are a loyal friend and will take a bullet for those you love, and in today's world, that is rare, unique, and hard to find – a true treasure. So, what do you say you and I take on this project? I will support you and you be successful at it.

"Alex, come on! I'm not going to buy your sad story. Your past doesn't define you, and it definitely doesn't serve you to keep holding on to it. What does serve you and define who you are, is your passion and love for what you do. So, my advice is to stay focused on what your vision is, and what you say you wanted to accomplish. Stay focused on that burning desire you have to complete this goal of yours and don't stop until you get it. No more second-guessing yourself. No more doubting yourself. I've got your back, and whenever you get stuck, know that I am here for you always."

These are some of the encouraging words from the people who inspired me when I was a young man.

In hindsight, I think what I love most about them is they were always calm about whatever was causing my fears and anxieties. They trusted the way life was going to unfold, as though they could see my future.

When I shared what I was experiencing, they were relaxed and so sure the outcome would be positive, as if they knew a secret about my life they were sharing with me indirectly, through their optimism.

That kind of assurance enabled them to be great listeners, vulnerable and compassionate with me. It made me seek them out whenever I had a challenge, whenever I couldn't see the forest past the trees, or whenever I needed to be reminded I had the ability to create my own solutions.

Inspirational people lift your spirits with their encouragement, love, compassion, and their abilities to be who you need them to be during challenging times.

They walk with you hand in hand, always supportive.

Their best gift to offer you is to paint a beautiful, heroic picture of you, bigger and more refined than the one you have of yourself.

I once told the people who inspired me: "I want to be able to see myself the way you see me."

I have shared this story with you so you can become that inspirational individual your kids so desperately need.

That higher vision has to come from somewhere and someone. If it's not created and projected for our kids to see themselves in a healthy and empowering way, the desire to be great slowly dies within them.

Then they will look to their peers to acknowledge them and give them the praise and recognition they so desperately need. That leads to being a follower, potentially following the wrong influencers.

If we don't satisfy their burning desire to be someone we can be proud of, then they will seek to self-medicate that incompleteness within them with alcohol, drugs, and other substances, developing abusive behaviors.

Being inspirational is an art form, a practice which you must commit to.

This is a conscious effort with a deliberate plan to create specific results with your kids.

The unconscious version leads you to *not* create a higher standard for your kids to reach for. In return, they unconsciously default to your lowest expectations of themselves.

My coach and mentor is one of the few inspirational people who come to my mind.

If you are blessed to have at least one living angel in a lifetime, hold onto that individual!

I met my coach/mentor when I was 23 years old. She not only spoke to my greatness, but she also fought for it. I still remember the battles.

I fought for my smallness and my limitations, while she fought for my greatness. I'm happy to say she won. Her love for me was stronger than mine, and she never gave up until I discovered I had a gift within me.

Her name is Sue Keith. She is an amazingly powerful woman, leader, mother, daughter, sister, aunt, and friend. Sue is one of the premier leadership development trainers in the country, helping people discover their own heartfelt leader within. I asked Sue to take part in my book.

Below is our dialogue:

What does it take to inspire our kids?

Lead by Example

I endeavor to inspire my kids by letting them see what I am up to in the world. To do that, I first needed to find the courage to step into my life's vision, and when I did, I invited my kids to be part of it. By including them in my commitment to follow my dreams, they were able to watch me discover my purpose in life.

I didn't want our kids to see my purpose as just a job. By exposing them to my life's journey, they saw how much work there was to be done in this world, and it gave them permission to find their own way of making it. I also wanted them to see the quality of relationships I build in my work, so they might be excited about doing the same.

Build a Supportive Village

I recognized it would take more than what I, alone, could offer. When I was a young parent, I realized I had been given two treasures, and I wanted to surround them with people who cheered them on with supportive and encouraging words; I wanted to create a village of people who saw the greatness in our children and assured them they could make a big difference in this world.

Return to Your Core

Lastly, framing our whole parenting style were two core factors: trust and respect. Throughout our kids' lives, those two factors have allowed me to walk hand-in-hand with my kids because the open flow of communication and trust painted me as the person to whom they can always turn.

Now my kids aren't kids anymore. They're in their late 20s. They have their own lives, and they're leaving their own marks in this world.

Where should I start on the journey to becoming an inspirational parent?

When our kids were young, my husband and I sat down to identify the core values we would impart to our children. We discussed the characteristics we wanted to model, as well as the messages we wanted our children to carry forward.

We decided we would consciously work to make our relationships with our kids their safe space. Outside of our relationships with them, we deliberately surrounded them with people who supported our values. Because family was our top priority, we made sure our kids spent plenty of time with their grandparents. Our family shared many multigenerational dinners, and when we needed a babysitter, we called Grandma and Grandpa, ensuring both sides of the family engaged with our kids often. These moments created many learning opportunities for our children, and without a conscious decision about our parenting style, our children wouldn't have been exposed to these vital lessons.

As our kids grew, we encountered challenges and trials in our parenting – moments when we questioned whether we were passing on the values and lessons we originally intended. The more I trusted the path we were on, however, the more we were consistent in our messaging. We trusted they would, eventually, adopt the messages we set out to teach them, and they did.

How do I shift my relationship with my children to become an inspiration?

As kids mature into teens and young adults, they begin to create their own picture of their lives, but that picture didn't always look like what I envisioned for them. That was difficult at first. As I surrendered my picture and gradually enrolled in their versions, however, our relationship really shifted.

I began to think about my role differently, and I looked for ways to fit into their picture, rather than forcing them to fit into mine. With this approach, I transitioned to their trusted confidant. They allowed me to ask questions, help them analyze their lives, and ultimately, influence them throughout their journey.

It's really amazing when they reach out to me, asking for my opinion or thoughts about the direction of their lives. It's as if the relationship has flipped; I'm now enrolled in their vision, as a mentor and a mother.

I had to surrender my picture, trusting who they are instead of what they are doing. I trust their abilities to weave their own paths, with all the ups and downs. They can figure out their own solutions. I don't have to force my agendas on them.

The biggest gift for me is being able to witness monumental moments in their self-discovery: when they recognize who they've become in their careers, or they find authenticity in their relationships. I could not be any more proud of them, and my pride comes from more than their accomplishments; it's much deeper. I am most proud of the amazing human beings they've become.

Describe your biggest leap of faith as a parent.

I had to acknowledge their path – and where it differed from mine.

My son, for example, had a gorgeous head of blond hair. In his teens, he decided to dye his hair black. It was one of those moments when I thought to myself: "Am I going to see this as a battle, or is it about personal expression and freedom?" I decided to ride it out.

He dyed his hair black, and then he got little snakebite piercings just in time for his high school senior pictures. I didn't make an issue of it. Next came the tattoos.

I kept thinking about how people would judge him – or how these choices would impact his ability to get a job. Until he was 18, he had to follow my ground rules.

Just before his 18th birthday, he came to me with a list of reasons as to why he wanted his first tattoo. He laid it out for me, addressing all of my fears and concerns. He agreed not to get any inappropriate tattoos that would show outside of a dress shirt.

Then it came to me: a moment of surrender. I acknowledged his ability to address my worries, as well as his desire to enroll me in his decision. He explained why it was important to him, and I got it. I respected this stop along his coming of age, and I saw the bigger picture – his ability to make a choice for himself, rather than acting out of rebellion. I honored that moment.

Today, he is a full expression of body art. He has a piece of his entire family painted somewhere on his body, and that process has totally flipped my point of view.

Navigating the fear of losing control over our kids is a dance. I don't want to be the parent who intervenes in my child's experience. But when do I hold my ground? When do I surrender? It's a process that takes on an ebb and flow, and it's part of letting our kids grow up. We allow them to make mistakes because we trust they'll learn from their breakdowns.

My daughter was in a progressing relationship, and she decided she wanted to live with her boyfriend. I had a rock solid stand: "Not before you're engaged and your commitment to walking down that aisle is imminent and apparent to us."

It wasn't about morality for me. There are so many special experiences on the other side of the wedding day, and one of the joys of being newlyweds is living together for the first time. I didn't want her to miss out on the specialness of marriage.

I stood my ground for a while, but she came back to address my issues with the decision. Like my son, she had her point of view written out, letting me know why it was important to her. She told me she didn't want her decision to move in with her boyfriend to become an act of defiance.

Pleased by how she handled the situation, I again surrendered. I honored her moment.

The experience taught her valuable lessons, and she learned things that supported her in her next steps in life.

Eventually, they decided living together wasn't going to work, and they ended their relationship. But she was better for the experience.

I learned my own lesson as a parent: Go for the bigger win!

The bigger win isn't always fighting for the immediate point. They are out there flapping those mighty wings of theirs, working those muscles, yearning to be independent and powerful. As a conscious parent, I want to honor that process by respecting their ability to have an adult dialogue that leads us to work through it together and create an empowering experience – rather than a defiant and divisive one.

When did you trust yourself as a parent?

I read an article that was a life-changer for me. It described a style of parenting: those who hover over their kids, protecting them from the risk of hurting themselves. These parents operate from the fear of what may happen, trying to block their children from all potentially negative situations. Immediately, I called my kids over.

"I've diagnosed myself," I said. "I'm a helicopter parent."

As parents, we would rather take on every bad experience – like heartbreak or loss or ridicule – than watch our kids go through them, even once. But in order to trust my kids – in or to take that giant leap of faith – I had to let them have their own experiences. I had to learn how to fall in love with their own idea of their lives. That article opened up so many possibilities for me, eventually leading me to realize I don't need to be omnipresent, getting in the way of their journey.

My kids will be just fine.

There was a bonus, too. When I finally unburdened myself from the responsibility of fixing everything, I found freedom. It was beautiful and liberating. And as a result of these breakthroughs, my husband and I are now able to identify ourselves as more than just parents to our kids. Our relationships with them have taken on new layers, each one exciting and fulfilling in its own way.

If I'm living in my fear and doubting my parenting, what advice can you give me?

There's a coach for that! When you can't figure out how to get out of your own way, a coach can help you identify when and how your fear is manifesting, as well as if factors other than fear are blocking you. Sometimes you need someone else to weigh in before you can fully let go and trust yourself as a parent.

If that option is unavailable to you, I would call upon the immortal words of Bob Newhart: "Just stop it!"

Consider the idea that how you spend your energy, and what you speak out into the universe, creates your reality. The more you speak of that fear and bring it into existence, the more it becomes a self-fulfilling prophecy. Instead, speak about your vision because the more we speak to that, and its possibilities, the more it manifests in your new reality.

From a parenting perspective, we have to get ourselves out of the way; otherwise, we are raising a whole generation of codependent kids who are afraid to express themselves. They're afraid to take on life because they're reliant on your permission and approval.

It's up to us, as parents, to recognize the moment when we transition our parenting. At some point, our kids need to discover that they are just as powerful, or more so, as us. Sometimes, the best way to support them is to push them out of the nest and trust you've taught them how to fly.

Sue Keith is one of the people I described at the beginning of this chapter, and she will forever be an inspiration to me because she bestowed upon me the gift of discovering my 'Greatness Glasses.'

When it comes to inspiring others, I must first be inspired myself. I have to find my own inspirational people to help light my own fire. Then I must follow my heart and chase my dreams.

You cannot inspire others if you're not inspired.

Inspiration is a fire lit inside of your gut that calls forth a new way of being, propelling you on a journey to reinvent yourself, so you can chase after your passions.

Another major component for inspiring others, including your kids, is practicing positive thinking.

Your paradigm has to be adamant and steadfast in the idea that every challenge has a solution. You must be resolution-oriented and proactive in all circumstances.

One of the greatest beliefs I have adopted as a young man and a student of leadership is that I am bigger than all of my circumstances. There is nothing I cannot adapt to, overcome, or find a solution for, even if I can't see it at that particular moment.

Using my abilities to be creative and think outside of the box develops a unique assuredness.

When your kids watch you navigate your life in such a manner, they can't help but be inspired by your confidence, poise, and resilience.

As I stated earlier in this chapter, when defining some of the character traits of my inspirational mentors, learning the art of raising one's spirit is an absolute must if you want to be influential in your kids' lives.

Now, let's identify a few lifestyle traits that can sabotage your efforts of inspiring your teens:

- Being a poor listener, hearing what you want rather than what is being said

- Projecting your fears and doubts onto your kids

- Not being present – distracted and aloof

- Unappreciative, not finding something to be grateful for

- Positioned, having a fixed mindset

- Reactive, quick to judge, and jumping to conclusions without facts

- Disappointed easily, not having enough compassion for a learning curve

- Resigned, giving up on your child's potential

- Harping on mistakes, unwilling to forgive and move on

- Pointing out things to correct or giving advice without creating permission

- Blaming and pointing fingers, not taking accountability

- Getting angry, frustrated, and losing your temper

- Raising your voice out of animosity

- Being impatient and causing a stressful environment

- Constantly bringing up the past

- Avoiding risk, playing it safe in life

- Constantly worrying about life and what could go wrong or when things don't go right

- Stressed constantly about things that are out of your control

- Doing just enough to get by

- Refusing to ask for help, stubborn

If you can relate to or acknowledge some of the above traits in your parenting, I invite you to commit to making the necessary changes to start winning over your son or daughter's trust.

If you feel you have evolved past these potentially limiting parenting traits, then I will give you some tips at the end of the chapter on how to be purposeful in your next level of inspirational parenting.

For now, I want to share one more contribution from a good friend. Patricia Villamil is a Transformational

Trainer for Hispanic communities across the country and a powerful owner at Mision Vital, a center for leadership development.

One of Patricia's strongest traits as a Transformational Trainer and owner is her ability to inspire others.

***

What does it take to be inspirational to others, in general? What does it take from you, specifically? How do you inspire young people?

In order to inspire other people, you have to learn how to be an authentic leader. You need to be 100% honest with who you are, speaking from that kind of truth, and ultimately, creating a space for others to trust you enough to reach out to you when they're in need.

As an inspirational leader, your goal is to be fluid, always seeking solutions, and optimistic of multiple outcomes of possibilities and success.

Sharing with others your authentic desire and vision to have them win gets people excited. It moves them and lifts them up from any hopelessness they may have otherwise.

What it takes from me to inspire others is to get out of my own way, to come from love, and believe they're more capable than they can ever imagine.

It requires enormous faith, trust, and encouragement. I have to be resilient in my conviction of their potential and keep standing for them – no matter what.

The best way to inspire young people is to be the example you want to see in them. Understand they have a gift, and they are a contribution to the world. Help them discover their voice, and let them know their voice matters and is important.

In order to be an inspirational parent, you must surrender your fear-based parenting style, which is also part of the controlling parenting style.

The controlling parenting style worked when your kids were little because they had no choice and no voice.

When they turn nine or ten and discover they have a voice, the moment calls forth a new parenting style, which is what I call the coaching/mentoring style.

Just before your kids turn twelve, you should be practicing how to be the coaching mom or dad they need.

Encouraging, empowering, and asking them open-ended questions draws out their greatness, so they can grow to be self-aware, self-assured, self-loving, and confident leaders.

With the coaching/mentoring parenting style, there is no room for fear to be rooted in your decisions as the leader in your family.

You will be surprised how much fear creeps into so much of your thoughts, your choices, and your actions.

When you are unconscious, you cannot see the depths of all of your fear. When you wake up and start living honestly and authentically, you can acknowledge the fear you embody and start to make that change.

As promised, here are a few tips to help you become that inspirational leader:

1. Encourage your kids. Find three to five encouraging phrases to say to them repeatedly, until they get tired of hearing it. I promise they won't. Here are a few examples:

   - You can do this, I know you can

   - You can figure this one out – trust yourself

   - I believe in you, and I trust you have what it takes

   - I have your back, and I'm here for you whenever you need me.

2. Give up the re-activeness in your parenting. You can borrow one of the mottos I use:

It is what it is. So what; now what? Find the solution.

Use this every day until you live by it, teach it, and pass it on to your kids.

3. Start the process of developing your 'Greatness Glasses'. Keep visualizing your teens as the powerful young adults you believe them to be, and keep painting that picture more vividly for both you and them. Then communicate that greatness to your kids.

4. Learn to let the past be the past. Don't keep dragging it into the present and tainting this new moment of unlimited possibilities for your kids to reinvent themselves.

5. Acknowledge your teenager. Find multiple things to acknowledge them for every day and every week until they get sick of all your praise. I promise they won't. Here are a few examples:

I am so proud of you; I learn so much from you – thank you for being my teacher

I appreciate the considerate and respectful young man you are becoming; I am in awe of the caring and compassionate young woman you are developing into.

DISTINCTION NINE
VULNERABILITY

This distinction and *way of being* is often avoided by most because, in order to be vulnerable, we must intimately and emotionally expose ourselves.

Vulnerability requires us to bring our walls down and allow people in, so we may be seen deeply by the ones we love the most.

Vulnerability takes a high level of trust in others, offering many blessings with some risk.

To be vulnerable with others, you need to risk feeling uncomfortable in certain situations. For example, you may have to risk rejection and belittlement.

It requires you to escape your comfort zone and be more courageous.

You must trust the people with whom you are vulnerable and have faith that they won't intentionally hurt you or take advantage of you.

The challenge for most people who want deep, meaningful relationships is overcoming the fear of opening themselves up. Allowing people in is the gateway for deep, meaningful relationships, and vulnerability is the birthplace. It's where all the magical moments are created.

Courage is your key to the gate, and fear must be conquered along the way.

Unless you have developed an extraordinary level of self-confidence and you know exactly who you are, the thought of being vulnerable in your relationships can appear to be a daunting and frightening experience.

However, when you attain higher levels of consciousness by fully loving and accepting yourself, you experience a sense of freedom to be as vulnerable as you choose with whoever you choose – without fear.

Vulnerability is the key to creating intimacy. It's the secret to connection.

Without your unwavering commitment to being completely vulnerable, you cannot know the depths of your ability to connect and create loving, fulfilling relationships.

Having relationships in which you deny vulnerability may feel shallow or one-dimensional.

Brene Brown has spent the last 15 years studying vulnerability and is a research professor at the University of Houston, Graduate College of Social Work. She has an amazing TEDx speech called, *The Power of Vulnerability*. She shares some powerful insight from her research and experiences.

"Connection is why we are all here; connection is what gives us purpose and meaning in our lives," Brene says. "We numb vulnerability."[2]

Remember this! We were all born as loving and vulnerable beings, but somewhere along our life's journey, we unconsciously decided to numb ourselves.

The pain and trauma some of us experience from our dysfunctional upbringings can be mentally and emotionally intolerable when we're young – too much for us to endure – so we numb ourselves to cope with the pain.

Remember, your ego's job is to protect you and keep you safe. The ego will do whatever it takes to block the pain that accompanies heartbreaks and disappointments.

Ego will build walls to keep us guarded and numb, so we don't feel the emotional anguish that comes with the risks of loving people.

When we numb ourselves, we no longer experience our vulnerability. Our natural state of vulnerability is no longer apparent to us. It faintly sits idle in the background, waiting for us to awaken from the unconscious sleep we have been accustomed to.

---

[2] https://goo.gl/LmAOpg

One of the downfalls to being numb is the inability to numb specific emotions. When we numb, we numb all feelings.

I want you to consider the possibility that, in your numbness, you cannot feel all the other amazing feelings to their fulfillment, such as joy, happiness, connectedness, appreciation, excitement, passion, and aliveness.

Is it no wonder we are constantly chasing external things to keep soothing that empty void we feel inside of us – the *doing* and the *having* – to *be* someone who is loved, appreciated or worthy, with a sense of belonging.

How does being vulnerable feel to you?

It makes me feel loved, honored, grateful, significant, and alive. More importantly, it validates that I am a compassionate, caring, and a loving human being.

I also know what it feels like to be numb, cold, shutdown, and unconsciously avoiding my vulnerability.

I had two awakenings in this area: one when I first realized my vulnerability as a young adult, and another when I discovered its power.

My second experience was more profound than the first.

I was in a banquet room at a graduation ceremony for my first transformational training, and there were about 120 people in attendance.

The facilitator asked our graduating class if anyone wanted to share their experience or value they had gained from the training.

I raised my hand and was asked to stand up and share.

I openly and candidly shared my amazing experience. As I shared how much I loved myself, how much I mattered, and how important it was for me to never let my kids stop loving themselves, I choked up, and my voice cracked. I became emotional thinking about how much I love my kids and want the absolute best for them.

Instead of holding back the emotions, I just surrendered.

I exposed my feelings and fully accepted how others perceived it.

When I sat down, I heard a thunderous applause that brought a smile to my face, validating I had been heard.

I was somewhat embarrassed because I had opened myself up, allowing myself to share and letting myself be truly vulnerable in a room full of strangers.

At the next opening (break?), I got up and urgently walked outside to get some fresh air. As I was sitting outside in the front of the building, I struggled with my ego because it didn't want me to go back in that room. In fact, if I had let my ego have its way, it would have had me jump in my car and drive straight home.

However, I chose to stay, overriding my ego and trusting my spirit.

When the event was over, about five people approached me and thanked me for sharing.

One man said, *"Hey man, I just want to thank you for sharing your story tonight with me. My wife has been begging me to join her in the next training as a way to save our marriage. We have been struggling in our relationship for a while, and I have been so reluctant to go with her.*

"After you shared tonight, I realized I could not share as you did," he continued. *"What I saw in your ability to open up, and share was the courage and vulnerability that is missing in me. I saw the part of me I feel I need to learn, so I can really show my wife how much she means to me and how much I love her.*

"You inspired me tonight, and because of you, I have signed up for the next training with her," he said. *"I wanted to thank you, and I hope to see you around."*

A young girl, who looked to be about age 18, thanked me for sharing, too: *"It's so beautiful to see a tough macho guy like you share from your heart. Your kids are blessed to have a loving father like you, who cares so much about them and is willing to make changes in himself to be a better dad for them.*

"I wish my dad had opened up and shared himself like that with me when I was younger," she continued. "If only he could have seen how much my siblings and I needed that from him. We never knew who he was because he never revealed himself to us. I don't think he even knew who he was.

"My Dad passed away a few months ago, and your story tonight made me think about how much I love him and miss him," she said. "I wish he could have shared with me a love as strong as you seem to have for your kids."

She and I stood there crying together, as dozens and dozens of people walked by us, but neither one of us cared. What was more important was the connection two strangers shared with each other because of the courage we both had that night to be vulnerable.

That night, my sharing, the feedback from strangers, and the vulnerability I experienced completely changed my life!

Since then, I have been rigorously committed to practicing *being* more vulnerable with people in my relationships, and it has brought me so many deep and meaningful moments shared with people, including the ones I love most.

Below are some new beliefs I have created about vulnerability:

- When I am willing to be vulnerable, people see the "real" (authentic?) me.

- Vulnerability is what our spirits yearn for, to make a meaningful connection.

- When I allow myself to be vulnerable, it gives others permission to be vulnerable, too.

- Vulnerability isn't a sign of weakness; it's a symbol of strength, love, confidence, and certainty.

- To be vulnerable is to feel alive, relevant, and fully present in the moment.

- When I'm vulnerable, it's easier for me to apologize and to give others the gift of serenity.

- Being vulnerable allows me to be empathetic toward others, not taking things personally.

- Fear fades when I'm vulnerable.

- I am a great listener when I am vulnerable.

- My vulnerability creates a safe space for others to open up and trust me effortlessly.

- People get inspired by my willingness to be vulnerable, mirroring to them its value.

- Vulnerability puts people at ease.

When I decide to be vulnerable with my kids, they respond compassionately. It gives them space to remember that is who they are.

Most people think vulnerability is a sign of weakness, being powerless or submissive. For me, it's one of the magical ingredients to creating extraordinary relationships in which one is courageously open, honest, and revealing.

If you are truly present in your relationships with your kids, you will see there are many openings to be vulnerable with them.

Now, here are two different scenarios where parents can seize the opportunity to create these powerful family moments of connecting deeply and honestly.

Scenario One:

You and your son get into an argument because you disagree with a decision he continually makes, and you feel he doesn't see the potential harm. Your son gets upset, runs off into his room, and slams the door.

As your ego tells you to continue with your activities, to unconsciously ignore what just happened, you avoid it or pretend it will just work itself out. Or worse, your ego comes up with all kinds of reasons to blame him: It's his fault that he doesn't get it, or he just wants to do what he wants to do because he is stubborn.

For dramatic effect, I will throw in: He is the son, and I am the parent; he should come to me and apologize.

Let's entertain the possibility that you have figured out how to turn your ego off. You have looked into your heart, connecting with your spirit. What would your spirit say?

"Alex, remember that you are responsible for the relationship. You are wiser and more advanced at relationships than he is. It's your job to teach him how to have disagreements in a healthy way, and it's up to you to clean it up. See this moment as an opportunity for both of you to learn how to be loving and accepting of each other's differences of opinion."

You stop what you're doing and knock on your son's bedroom door. He says, "Come in." You walk in his room with the intention of being vulnerable, authentic, and completely honest with him.

You say to him: "I'm sorry if I hurt your feelings, offended you, or made you feel bad and wrong for your decision. I reacted out of fear because I am afraid you are going to hurt yourself – or worse. I shouldn't project my own fears onto you.

You are my son. I love you with all of my heart, and you mean the world to me. If anything ever happened to you without me helping you make better choices, I don't know if I could forgive myself.

I need to learn how to communicate honestly with you instead of letting my fear get to me and react the way I did. I hope you can forgive me, and see all I want is the best for you. I want you to make the best decisions for yourself. I only want to be your partner in helping you make smart choices and share my wisdom with you."

Open your arms to receive a hug.

Your son replies, "Thank you for that. I never considered your feelings or how you can be affected by my decisions. It really opened my eyes to see your point of view, and I really do want to make better choices for myself.

I will really consider your opinion and take into account that maybe your way is safer. I'm sure there is a compromise in my options somewhere, where we can find a win/win for us both."

If you are cringing as you read this, it's probably because you cannot see yourself being this way with your kids or speaking to them like this – or them speaking like this to you.

Before my own conscious awakening, I could not see this for myself or my family either, but I promise you it is possible, and emotionally healthy-hearted and mindful people really do create these kinds of powerful moments with their kids.

Scenario Two:

You and your daughter are sitting in the living room. She says something to you, but you don't hear her. Your daughter says, "Hello … are you listening to me?" You say, "I'm sorry what?" She says, "Never mind," and storms off.

Before she leaves the living room, you tell her: "Wait, come back." She stops for a moment, rolls her eyes, huffs, puffs, and pouts. She says, "What?"

"I'm really sorry for ignoring you," you say. "It's not about you. I have a lot on my mind. Come sit next to me, and I will share with you."

Your daughter makes a beeline to the couch to sit next to you because she sees an opportunity to be there for you.

When she sits down, you prepare to bring your walls down and let her in by mustering up the courage to trust your whole heart with her.

"They started laying off people at work today, and one of my closest friends just got let go today. I am both sad for him and nervous for myself, and I haven't been as present as I should be," you share. "Anyway, I want you to know I wasn't ignoring you on purpose. I guess I have been letting the worry take over me, and I need to learn how to let it go."

Your daughter grabs your hand and says, "I'm sorry you are going through that. I didn't mean to snap at you. I didn't realize you could be going through some challenges, or take into consideration that you have a lot on your mind."

"I guess I never really think my parents have their struggles and challenges because they always appear to have everything under control," she continued.

"Thank you for sharing this with me. I want you to know I love you and appreciate all the sacrifices you both make for Tommy and me, so we can live the life you have provided for us."

Hugging opportunities exist at this moment for you both if you create it and/or take it.

Most kids are not evolved or enlightened enough yet to be the one to create that kind of opening, to *be* that invitation, to *be* that space for you guys to experience this kind of relationship.

That's why it is imperative that you take responsibility for the relationship and teach them how to create these kinds of connections and moments from your example and efforts.

If someone in your family is trying to create that for you, and you are the one who doesn't seem to want to trust and fall in line with them, I hope this is your wake-up call!

If you read the scenarios, and you could never in a million years believe you and your kids could have that kind of dialogue, you are mistaken. It is quite possible.

One of the ways people often get stuck when learning to think positively is not to believe what is possible, or not having the capacity to see things as a possibility in the first place – with or without evidence. That why it's called believing.

I promise it is possible, and highly probable, that you can and will create any kind of relationship you are committed to. Your commitment and follow through will be the difference.

Okay, let me take a moment to address the fear most people have of being hurt by the people we choose to be vulnerable with.

To be truly vulnerable, must you risk the possibility of getting hurt? Yes!

Not only do you have to risk it, but you must also experience the pain if it happens.

If you are going to be in the game called relationships, expect to be hurt or feel pain many times. It's par for the course.

Ask any avid dog lover and rescuer if they are prepared to be bitten by a scared dog while trying to help them, and they will say: absolutely. They know it's part of the process.

So, if you want to be successful in relationships and don't want to feel pain, be rejected, or be judged, you're in the wrong game.

From my experience, when it comes to being vulnerable with kindhearted people, the rejection, the ridicule, the betrayal, almost never occurs.

What I also have learned about people in the process of discovering my own vulnerability is most people are loving, compassionate, and kindhearted.

They don't really want to hurt you, and most of the time, when I do feel hurt by them, it's almost always the way I have misinterpreted their intentions.

There truly is something magical about being vulnerable around other kindhearted people – they respond!

Vulnerability is like a spiritual language only our souls know how to speak, an incredible love energy that invites the compassionate ones to step up and reveal their hearts.

Here is a great story I found on the internet that warmed my heart, and it really helps me paint a better picture of the power of vulnerability[3].

One day I was sitting around with a group of women after an exercise class. First, let me preface this with: I am a cool person. I am stoic. I am funny. I am positive. When I'm negative, I usually keep it to myself or tell a close friend.

---

[3] http://thisisimperfect.org/blog/2014/6/4/your-stories-on-vulnerability

Ok, so anyway... one day in this circle, after class, I was feeling that gnawing ache in my stomach of knowing I was disconnected with my husband. My kids were little, and I didn't know if I was an adequate mother to them or not. I had tried everything to lose weight, and it wasn't coming off. I knew I was inadequate in the eyes of our culture because of my fatness.

Then, almost inexplicably, a little earthquake began to rumble in the center of my being.

The women, maybe 10 of us, were all in a circle, and a few were having side conversations.

Tears started rolling down my cheeks. I could see a couple of women noticed, and they all elbowed each other until all eyes were on me.

This was when a full-on, unrestrained, outpouring of pain began. Before I knew it, I was sobbing and shaking, trying to explain, but I couldn't even talk. I was absolutely incapacitated by this. I could barely breathe. The women on either side of me had taken my hands in theirs, and this is when one of the most amazing things another human being has done for me happened.

I went to pull my hand away to wipe the torrential flow of snot off my face. While this woman, an acquaintance whose name I don't even remember, took her sleeve and wiped that grossness from my face, without a flinch, in a split second, and it was the kindest, most selfless thing I can recall anyone ever doing for me!

I left, and surprisingly, I was too humiliated to ever go back to this exercise class. However, the compassion of these women, particularly the lady beside me, had an enormous impact on me that day, and it changed me forever.

My life has gotten so much better since that one dark day. I'm divorced, thin, and more confident than I have ever been in my entire life. I like to think I pay it forward now.

I would love to have a chance to wipe someone's snot one day if they ever needed it. It was a powerful gesture. It made me feel safe enough to be an utter failure and an outright mess.

However, to walk away from that experience and grow as a direct result of the love I received from a group of compassionate strangers was a life lesson I will never forget.

As I wrap up this chapter, I hope I was able to open up a possibility for you to see the tremendous value you can create for yourself, your children, and the relationship you share together.

Remember, relationships are about relating with one another. Relating is defined as making or showing a connection between each other.

It doesn't take much effort to make a connection. That's what most of us are *doing* unconsciously in our lives by default.

But in order for you and your kids to make a deep, meaningful connection that is truly inspirational, that creates a trusting bond that allows you to be influential in their life, you must first elevate yourself to the next level of vulnerability; you have to master your ability to *be* vulnerable.

Here are a few suggestions to practice vulnerability:

- Create a guideline to help you open up and share honestly, reminding you to not hide behind anything. Give up the facade that your ego wants you to portray.

- Share the root cause of how you are feeling and why rather than hiding it, holding it in, or ignoring it and pretending that it's not important or doesn't matter. You could be feeling: afraid, nervous, concerned, sad, worried, insecure, doubtful, resigned, etc.

- When you share, give yourself permission to experience the emotion that is naturally associated with the feeling. Allow yourself to authentically express that emotion as you are sharing and feeling it.

- Constantly check in with yourself, noticing more and more how numb you have become, as well as how insensitive you are as a coping mechanism to the things you have decided not to feel. Decide those feelings are ways to remind you that you are a loving, caring, and compassionate parent.

DISTINCTION TEN
HONESTY

There is so much to write about on this topic when it comes to having integrity in your life, but what I'm going to talk about, specifically, is being honest with your feelings, which is also referred to as emotional honesty.

Emotional honesty means to be able to express your true feelings, by first acknowledging and admitting to the feelings or emotions you're experiencing.

Some people aren't even experiencing their experiences – nonetheless being honest about them. They're not that conscious, yet; instead, they are totally unaware. A lot of people are emotionally shut down. They have been for years, and they don't even know it.

Many people have stopped feeling their feelings years ago, and they haven't realized how much of an impact that has in the interest of creating extraordinary relationships.

However, that won't stop most people from putting a smile on their face, projecting to the world that everything is just great.

To be emotionally honest, you would first have to be emotionally aware of all of your senses and really be in tune with how you feel in each and every moment, as well as in relationship to all that you experience in life.

It's so important to be honest with your feelings when it comes to empowering and inspiring your children.

Being honest with your kids and sharing your feelings and true emotions with them actually levels the playing field for the both of you to engage in the relationship. Your honesty makes a statement to them that you are human, just like they are.

It says to them you do have feelings, you do get afraid, you do get nervous, you do worry, and from time to time, you don't have all the answers – just like them.

You have no idea how important that is in the relationship with your kids. I only know this because, in the teen training, this is what teens tell me. What they want most is for their parents to stop trying to act like they have it all under control, and be honest.

There is an old-school sales technique I learned about 20 years ago, which I have enjoyed using with people. I don't use it to sell them anything. I use it to get them to open up and connect with me.

It has been so effective with my clients and in my business. I most commonly teach it to all of my parent clients to use with their kids.

The technique is called: "Feel, Felt, and Found."

This is what it sounds like:

"I know how you feel."

"I have felt the same way."

"What I have found is..."

I know how you feel implies you understand the feeling they may be experiencing. *I have felt the same way* implies you, too, have felt that way, and now you both have that in common. *What I have found is* implies you now have some valuable insight because you have been down that road before.

What makes this technique so effective when communicating with your kids is it starts off by immediately letting your kids know you, too, have felt what they feel, and you are empathetic to what they are feeling, as well.

Being empathetic to what they are going through is the first stage to opening them up; it demonstrates that you understand or are acknowledging their process. It reassures them that what they are feeling is valid, and it's okay that they are feeling this way.

Most of the time, as parents, we skip this stage in the process of them sharing with us, and we go straight into offering them advice or sharing our points of view. When we do that, it sends the message that we're not listening to them, and we make it about our agendas and wanting to fix the problem.

It implies to them we don't care how they feel, and from their point of view, it affirms all we really care about is our own needs, making it all about us.

This is why they get frustrated with us and storm out of the room, saying, "Ugh … you never listen to me!"

When we authentically affirm we have felt the same way, it lets them know we are being honest with them about our feelings – that we trust them enough to bring our walls down, letting them in. It's like saying, "You're not alone."

The reason why this is so important is it shows them you're starting to bring down your defenses, and it's safe to engage. In return, it gives them permission to bring their walls down and let you in.

More importantly, it gives them permission to turn off the buffers on their ears, allowing them to open up, ready to hear anything you have to say. It's a powerful tool when you're applying it from a place of being authentic and vulnerable.

The best part of this process is, after you have revealed yourself to them, they now trust you, and they open themselves up to hear all the wisdom you have to share.

It may be a short window that temporarily has been opened up, but nevertheless, it's open now, and you created it. So, this is where you have to make it count.

As a statement, "What I have found" is a pathway for you to share your own realizations, your own breakthroughs, or learning experiences. Here is where you get to plant some powerful seeds of learning for them to cultivate, through your story sharing abilities.

When you share your message along this path, it is more likely to be perceived from their point of view as a powerful insight, a great lesson, or great advice they need to remember to better themselves, versus hearing it from the perspective that you are trying to tell them what to do, or you want them to do it your way.

What I love most about this amazing communication tool is it opens people up authentically, to hear what you have to contribute from a neutral place, without them thinking there are any hidden agendas or alternative motives. It's pure.

The magical ingredient this process uses, making it so effective, is your willingness to first be vulnerable. When you are 100% honest with your own feelings – sharing your story and the lessons you've learned – in such a way, it plants seeds within them that will sprout in their own time, letting the wisdom take effect when needed.

Another reason why being honest with your feelings is so important is it gives your kids permission, to be honest with you about how they feel.

Isn't that what you want?

I don't know why, but for some reason, I've noticed all it takes is for one person in a group of two or more people to be so courageously honest in their sharing that it seems to cause other people involved in that communion to open up, trust, and share deeply.

It's a relationship phenomenon.

If you have ever been in a support group setting, with a facilitator who has the right context to open up a safe, loving, and non-judgmental space for emotionally honest sharing, you would know what a powerful, moving, and inspiring experience that can be.

All people genuinely want to be open, intimate, and deeply connected in their relationships, but most people seem to be waiting for someone else in the relationship to *be* it first – to be the space for it to happen in, to create the space, and *be* the invitation to start it.

Here are a few of the challenges I've realized when it comes to people being emotionally honest.

Most of us like to think we're honest human beings when it comes to interacting with others in our relationships. However, what I've learned is most of us are not so honest when it comes to what, or how, we "really" feel.

Hear me out for a minute.

There are those of us parents who want and yearn for our kids to be so open and honest with us in our relationships, yet we unconsciously hold back from sharing with them how we truly feel.

It's not because we don't want to. In our own unconsciousness, our ego forbids it. We don't realize that we're not being honest, or another possibility is some of us don't know how to effectively articulate how we truly feel.

Who taught you how to communicate your feelings?

A lot of us have never really learned how to put the right words together to accurately describe, convey, or express how we really feel.

The last possibility is some of us are just numb and don't really feel anything anyway. Some of us are emotionally shut down, disconnected from our own feelings, afraid to feel the pain that relationships can dish out.

You will be amazed how many times I've asked people, "How does that make you feel?" They will answer: good, fine, or I feel ok, not realizing those are not feelings.

I remember one day going to a baseball game with a good friend of mine who is an analyzer personality: very intelligent. However, from my perspective, I sometimes struggle with interpreting how he feels because it's not always so apparent.

I remember the game was so much fun, filled with home runs, high fives, lots of excitement, and cheering. Our team won!

As we were both walking back to the car, I felt alive and filled with team spirit, camaraderie, joy, and excitement. I had a little extra bounce to my step.

I looked over at my friend, and I said, "Are you having a good time?" He looked back at me and said, "Yes, I am."

"Well, you might want to tell your face because your face doesn't know that yet," I replied.

Both of us laughed hysterically.

When we got back to the car, I had a theory of why it's not always apparent to me when my friend is enjoying himself, physically, emotionally, or spiritually.

So, I shared my theory with him: "Could it be possible you don't fully experience your experiences anymore – the way you used to when you were younger?"

My friend pondered for a moment, then he looked at me and said, "Yes."

"Could it also be possible that you have conceptualized your experiences in your head, rather than actually giving yourself permission to feel them?" I asked.

My friend again pondered for a moment. He looked at me and said, "Yes."

As we drove home from the baseball game, my friend and I had a long discussion about the possibility that, when he was younger, he could have unconsciously shut down his feelings and emotions to avoid the pain, disappointment, and sadness in his childhood.

He shared with me that he never really learned how to express himself in a healthy way when he was younger. He definitely didn't feel safe enough within his own home to experience the emotions he was feeling, he shared, let alone reveal those findings with anyone in his family.

Imagine what your relationships would look like if only you were so bold in your efforts and commitment to feel and reveal yourself so courageously – freed up to admit your own fears, to own up to your own doubts and your own insecurities with your kids. What then would be possible?

What I know to be possible, and highly probable for you as a parent is you would truly inspire your children through your own vulnerability and virtuous efforts.

Honesty reveals to them that you are open and exposed, sending them the message that you trust them with your heart, and you can truly be trusted.

They, in return, would soon learn for themselves to trust you again, and a magical moment would unfold right before your eyes as they begin to open up to you, revealing themselves wholeheartedly.

When they trust you again, they will seek your advice, guidance, wisdom, and support.

All you have been trying to force out or pull from your kids would all of a sudden open itself up to you, and it would all come from a courageous commitment to surrender your fears – letting go of your ego, getting real with yourself, and putting all of your trust into them.

Honesty is what it takes from you to re-engage and reconnect with your son or daughter in such a way that hooks their heart. They will trust you enough to take a chance with you, re-inventing a new and improved relationship that is healthy and promising.

I have helped many parents cause a profound shift in the relationship with their teenagers; some have done a 360-degree turn within days, depending on the severity of cleanup work and healing that needs to take place for this kind of change to occur.

Not to mention, in my own relationship with my kids, I've seen so much change in all the years I have been practicing my ability to *be* real with them. I've learned to just be honest with them as to how I am truly feeling, what I am afraid of, or what my concerns are.

It requires me to deeply trust that being honest with my kids about my own feelings will always deliver a compassionate response. It will always produce empathy and a deeper level of understanding as they find something they can relate to.

Each one of my kids has a piece of my heart because I gave it to them a long time ago. I am proud to say they have taken good care of it thus far, treating my honest sharing as though it's a precious offering.

I empower you to think of it as though you're giving your kids a rare, unique, one-of-a-kind, and irreplaceable gift, and they get to decide its true value for themselves, inspiring them to take good care of it and cherish it forever.

My kids really seem to appreciate that gift. They feel honored, and they handle it with such care and dignity.

Oh, and let me remind you that your ego won't let you believe any of this, and it will do everything it can to talk you out of what it calls nonsense. If you're still reading, however, I know that you know, deep inside your spirit, none of this is nonsense. It's none other than the language of love.

Your spirit always knows the truth – listen to that.

Remember your ego's job is to keep you safe and protect you from pain, so the last thing it wants you to do is to reveal yourself so honestly. It's afraid your kids might use it against you, ultimately hurting you in the process.

I had to be willing to trust that this kind of honesty would connect us deeply to each other, strengthening our bond, reaffirming the love we have for one another, and reminding us we have so much in common.

I had to surrender the egoic fear that my kids were that dark, cruel or malicious. I had to believe and trust that they are my little angels and that they operate from love, like me.

One of the most powerful exercises I facilitate in my teen training is a process where everyone gets a chance to identify with and acknowledge their own feelings at pivotal moments in their life.

What makes the exercise so profound is most teenagers think they are the only ones feeling the way that they do, and when they realize other teens feel, or have felt, the exact same way, it creates this powerful and trustworthy bond within the group.

This exercise creates the context of trust and is the framework for the training to build upon, opening the space for acceptance, deep and intimate sharing, compassion, togetherness, and partnership – a true feeling of oneness.

When I use the exercise in the Teen and Parent Training, there is not a dry eye in the room. It's the most powerful and profound experience I have ever had the privilege to be a part of, so I know it works. I just want it to work for you, in your relationships and in your life.

It's not uncommon to hear teens share they feel closer to the group than they do with their own family. That's the most heartbreaking part of the exercise because it tells me this kind of honest sharing, deep connection, and bond is not happening at home with the ones they claim to love the most.

This tells me we, as a society, are deeply disconnected from our families.

I have racked my brain for years trying to figure out why this kind of honest sharing is so powerful.

I've only been able to conclude, so far, it is the honesty and openness of one's self that seems to inspire others to also be so bold in their own honesty, revealing more and more of their true selves.

This, in return, creates permission for all who are within an arm's distance of each other to bring down their walls and connect.

Upon writing this chapter, I thought I would reach out to my own kids and ask them how they feel about my ability to be open and honest with my feelings as their father.

Here are their responses.

Sasha Urbina, 21

When you are being honest with me with all of your own fears – or even when you are straightforward with me in sharing stories about how you grew up – I instantly feel relieved.

You are always honest and always wanting to be a part of my life, and willing to listen, so it's hard for me not to get emotional when we have meaningful conversations.

I know you are being real about all of your feelings, so I naturally open up about all of mine. I feel that our discussions are the most meaningful because you have brought authenticity to all of our conversations, and we have a type of relationship that is truthful – and that is special to me.

You help me see things when I can't, when I am unaware, with that I feel like I know myself most when you are around."

Love you Dad,

Sasha

Jazmine Urbina, 22

You've taught me that creating successful relationships can only happen when I'm willing to be open and honest with my feelings. From watching you, I've learned that it takes more than just honesty to be successful in that. It takes a lot of courage, too. What I didn't realize was that I had to be willing to make myself vulnerable in order to have deeper relationships that are more meaningful.

I think that, by watching you practice this every day, I picked pieces of it up unconsciously, but there is still more for me to learn. Having you constantly reminding me how to be vulnerable and seeing you do it, almost every day, seems a little bit less scary, and I'm practicing not being afraid of expressing myself.

As a daughter, I can't imagine growing up differently or raising children differently now that I know what it looks like to be a conscious parent, one who is present and pays attention.

I've realized the importance of being hyper-aware of their feelings and the things that they choose to share, either in words or in actions.

As a parent, it's critical that I remember what I needed as a teen and young adult in order to lead them. One of the things I needed was parents who weren't afraid, to be honest and had the courage to be vulnerable first, so I had permission to be and do the same."

Love,

Jazmine

Mark Urbina, 27

As your son, I always loved how open and honest you were with me as I grew up. To have a father who told me, "I love you, son," or "I'm proud of you," was definitely something I took for granted as a kid.

However, as I got older, I realized our father/son relationship was so different than many of my friends' relationships with their fathers.

I realized that you were my best friend growing up, and not too many kids can say that about their parents. When I say "best friend," I don't mean you would let me do whatever I wanted – because you didn't. That's what some kids call a "cool parent," letting them do whatever they wanted.

Dad, you were my best friend in other ways. You were supportive. You were present and attentive, always interested in me, asking questions. You pushed me to be my best. You taught me valuable lessons. You were an open ear to talk to, and there are other countless ways about you that really made me feel loved, safe, and uplifted!

Just like any other best of friends, we also had our ups and downs, and/or disagreements, but one thing I could always say is that I respected you no matter how close we got. I never forgot you were my father.

I think most parents get confused and are either the "Cool Parents" or the super strict overbearing parents, and that line is blurred sometimes.

One thing I loved about our relationship was that I always knew, no matter what I did, you always loved me. That was always comforting to know that no matter how bad I messed up, I had a rock-solid core that was supportive – and that you always had my back.

My earliest memories of you were when we would play sports together. From playing basketball, one on one, or you playing quarterback and throwing footballs at me until the sun went down and the lights turned off!

You were always pushing me to be better and making sure I never gave up, no matter how hard it was. I remember you once told me we're not leaving till I caught 100 footballs in a row. We were out on the field for hours until I finally caught every single ball!

I remember being so frustrated and hating you at that moment for pushing me and telling me to never quit, but as soon as I reached that goal of a 100, I had this huge smile on my face – I felt unstoppable.

I remember walking back to the car dead tired, but my confidence level was through the roof, and you asked me, "What did you learn?" A question you still ask me to this day.

I remember we laughed, and I told you: "I'm the best wide receiver in the world, and I can catch anything you throw at me!"

That moment was huge for me because you pushed me and made me into the champion I am today!

I realized you can push someone from a loving place. You can take a stand for their greatness, and they will know in their heart your intentions are pure.

As my father, you were never scared to show me how you felt, and I always respected that about you. You showed me that it's ok to cry as a man, that it's ok for me to feel my feelings, and not care what anyone thinks.

That to me is something you never learn in school, or through friends. It's something I learned by watching you grow, be willing to share so openly like that, and become the amazing father that you are.

I can honestly say you are my hero, and I'm so proud of your accomplishments and your relentless need to change the world!

You inspire me to keep pushing and to follow my own dreams. I hope one day I will have as big of an impact on the world as you have."

Love you, Pops!

Mark Urbina

Wow! It really warms my heart to read those. When I asked them to send me a few thoughts about my openness and honesty, I never imagined it would have been so touching and heartwarming. I am forever grateful to be blessed with these three amazing children.

If you are willing to invest some courage, commitment, and vulnerability to reveal yourself more with your kids, they will be truly inspired by what you have shown them and the relationship you were willing to create with them.

Here are some tips to help you be more emotionally honest with your kids:

Instead of starting by telling your kids what you don't like them doing, or what they shouldn't be doing, try starting by asking them permission to share your concerns with them. When they say yes, open yourself up and be honest with them about your concerns.

For example: "My concern is, up until now, you have not shown me you are responsible enough to take on that task, and my fear is you will take it on anyway – without taking into consideration what kind of commitment it will require. Are you willing to have an adult conversation about it, so you set yourself up to win?"

If you are honest enough to admit you made a mistake, clean it up with an emotionally honest apology and explanation. Slowly, it should start to inspire them with your courage and honesty, making them feel that they can trust you more. You're also setting the example for future interactions with you.

For example: "Good morning, Brooklyn. I owe you an apology. I shouldn't have snapped at you last night. I'm so sorry. It wasn't your fault that I was mad. All of my own fears came up for me at that moment, and I realize I can't control every move you make. I have to just let you make some of those mistakes and learn for yourself. I'll be here to help you through the process. I love you." (Offer a hug.)

If you are feeling emotional and feel like crying, give yourself permission to cry. Trust that your courage, and confidence in who you are, will reveal itself in time. Set the emotional example that crying can be a healthy and healing experience when it's allowed to be expressed. After you have finished crying, share what you were feeling.

For example: "It breaks my heart to see you suffering, and I don't know what to do anymore. I'm just feeling emotional because I have been ignoring these feelings for so long, and it's time for me to deal with them. There is sadness and frustration in my heart; however, now that I have let them go, I can find the clarity to support you the way you need to be supported. Thanks for allowing me the freedom to express myself without judging me. I love you and appreciate you for that."

DISTINCTION ELEVEN
AFFECTIONATE

It's been said that people don't care how much you know until they know how much you care. I have found this saying to be true when it comes to teenagers and their relationship with their parents.

In order to be influential in the lives of your children, they must know you absolutely, unequivocally, love and care for them.

Simply telling your children you love them may not necessarily be enough for some kids. They may need more action, more proof.

Loving someone, and having that individual feel and experience your love, may be a more elaborate process than you considered.

It may require more than your words and actions for your love to be experienced how it was intended.

I'm not saying you don't love your child. I am saying perhaps some children need additional effort from you to actually experience your love for themselves.

Technically, love is only a word until it's fully expressed and well received from the person you intend to share your love. On their end, they may need to feel it and have an experience associated with your heartfelt declaration.

You don't know how many times I have had parents say to me, "I love all my kids exactly the same. I don't know why Timmy thinks I don't love him."

Most of us only show or express love in a few ways, but not every child perceives love in the same way. We all have our own love language, but in order to create an effective connection with all of your children, you must learn the love language to each of their individual hearts.

Loving people may not be as easy as you might think. Loving people from your end is one part of the process; expressing it in a way they need to be experienced is the second part of the process.

One of the most heartbreaking moments in the training room is hearing teenagers pouring their hearts out candidly, honestly, and courageously amongst their peers. They are not convinced their parents love or care about them.

I hear those cries from the healthiest, most nurtured, cherished child to the super abandoned, neglected, and often overlooked. They all come to the same conclusion: doubting their parents love for them.

How could this be? How could any child ever be uncertain of their parents' love? How does this even happen? Who do I need to *be* to change it?

Let's review a few possibilities as to why your kids may be disillusioned about your love for them.

Most parents are unaware of two components of human development. If they were aware and made the proper adjustments in their parenting, it would cause a profound shift in humanity and make the kind of difference with your children that breeds healthy, confident, and productive young men and women in our communities.

The first component:

The reality of human beings is based on our beliefs. We all have our own belief system, and once we believe something to be true, we act as though that belief is the truth.

We then seek other situations and scenarios in our life to affirm and validate it; therefore, we reinforce its legitimacy.

The problem with this paradigm is that some of our beliefs are negative and/or limited to our growth potential, keeping us from being open to new possibilities and, ultimately, creating new results.

Here is an example: Your son or daughter ask you an important question at a time when you are distracted, worried, or focused on something else. Your response was: *"Not right now. Give me a few minutes."*

Most likely, your child felt invalidated, unheard, and possibly rejected.

What most human beings do – especially kids – when we don't fully understand something is make up a belief about what happened. For example:

- What I have to say to you is not important

- My dad doesn't care about me

- My mom never has time for me

- No one cares what I have to say

If this experience happens a second time or a third time, your son or daughter would validate and affirm such beliefs are true – even if that was never your intention.

Those limiting beliefs now block you and your child's ability to connect. As long as your kids believe you don't care about what they have to say, they will slowly shut down, stop sharing with you, and slowly disconnect.

That will frustrate you more and lead you to create your own personal beliefs about them:

- He's just an angry person

- She doesn't want to open up to me; she's stubborn

- They don't listen to me

- None of them care; they just want to do it their way

The limiting belief is the root cause that keeps your kids from opening up, trusting, sharing, and knowing you still love and care for them.

Remember our beliefs shape our reality. When we live consciously, we distinguish the difference between what beliefs we might have versus reality.

I hope you can start making a more conscious effort to be more present with your kids. Give them the undivided attention they deserve, or at a minimum, learn how to communicate more honestly, in a way that communicates your true intentions.

The second component:

This is one of the most powerful tools you have in your parenting tool belt. It affirms that you do, indeed, care about them and love them with all your heart. That tool is affection.

Don't let affection be just another word you use to describe your relationships. Learn how to be affectionate and create an experience for yourself and another.

Have you ever been taught how to be affectionate? If so, who taught you?

If you were to ask your kids or spouse to rate your ability to be affectionate with them, how would they score you?

Affection is not a concept; it is the loving act of expressing your heartfelt emotions with one another. The dictionary defines affection as readily feeling or showing fondness or tenderness.

Some of us parents are challenged when it comes to authentically feeling our feelings or experiencing our experiences, and some of us are challenged when trying to express them. Some of us are challenged with both.

For many, it takes an enormous amount of courage and self-assurance to show our kids this side of us. It is an intimate practice, an honest and humble way of being; it requires a tremendous amount of trust.

What kind of trust? It requires trust that the people we reveal ourselves to won't:

- Hurt me
- Reject me
- Ignore me
- Take advantage of me
- Humiliate me

- Manipulate me

- Judge me

- Use it against me

- Abandon me

This is a side of you that you don't often share. For some of you, it's a side you don't allow yourself to access, yet this is what your kids need most from you.

They yearn for it. Their little souls crave this kind of connection with you. It is a vital component to the foundation of building a healthy and nurturing relationship with your child.

Affection seems to be a lost art in today's world. I notice today's parent seems to be more concerned about correcting their kids' actions than giving them the emotional and physical affection they need to enrich their lives and build up their self-esteem.

We seem to want to control our children, give them advice, point out where they are falling short, or tell them the things we think they need to hear, rather than being who they need us to *be* for them to learn and grow into powerful young leaders.

When you muster up the courage and audacity to show your tenderness, compassion, vulnerability, and warmth to your kids, they will receive many blessings from it, and so will you.

Here are some of the benefits of being affectionate with your child:

- Creates a stronger connection between parent/child

- Develops a higher self-esteem for your child

- Creates a more fearless and well-rounded child

- Increases your child's brain development and memory

- Makes them physically healthier

- Helps a child's mental well-being

- Enhances parent-child communication

- Decreases psychological and behavioral problems

- Improves academic competence

- Heals some of their pain

As human beings, we need physical touch. Our kids need it because it offers comfort, reassuring that we are there for them.

Physical touch lets our kids know they can relax. It gives them some relief from the stresses they create for themselves and offers them some peace.

Children who receive plenty of affection have lower cortisol levels as they become adults. Cortisol is the stress hormone that creates anxiety and fear.

I recently read a study about teenagers, referring to their academic success. It stated that one of the most effective parenting models was the combination of an authoritative parenting style, in which guidance is firm and reliably consistent, accompanied by a high degree of emotional warmth and affection.

As a father of three beautiful children, and having lost a father to cancer, I want to share this short story with you; I hope it inspires you the way it inspires me.

My Dad's Hands

As I sit here praying to God on behalf of my father, I thank God for my dad's hands. Ever since I can remember, I knew my dad was unlike other dads. My dad would use his hands to help me in ways that other kids never experienced.

When I was little, his hands were big and strong. He walked me into school, my hand in his, which always made me feel safe, secure, and protected.

As I got older, he would use his hands to rub my head or touch my shoulder, always communicating to me that I am special, that he loves me, and that he recognizes me in those moments; it was a gift he gave me that was often overlooked.

When I didn't make the baseball team because I thought I wasn't good enough, it was overshadowed by his hand on my back, massaging me oh so gently as I cried, revealing that I was good enough for him.

Somehow, his hands would communicate things to me that no words could express. My dad's hands reminded me that I was loved, that he cared, that I was needed and wanted by him.

On my wedding day, it was the hands of my dad that reminded me of the loving husband I aspired to become, as he wiped the tears of joy from my mother's eyes.

It was my dad's hands that I saw holding my son hours after he was born, feeling a deep sense of love, compassion, and joy, only to realize that they were mine.

It was my dad's hands that I would recognize as I embraced my two beautiful little girls on my lap, holding them tight, bouncing them around playing horsey, laughing, and carrying on as little kids should.

My dad's hands were always there in moments of compassion, in moments of caring, in moments of comfort, in moments to heal.

From cleaning the blood of a scraped knee to holding them tight through a thunderstorm, my dad's hands were now mine.

And now, as I sit here praying to God for my father who is battling cancer, I have his hands in mine, feeling grateful and honored to be there for him the way he has been there for me – thanking him for all of his love, all of his support, and all of his affection.

Thank you, Dad, for showing me how to convey my love, to express it wholeheartedly, to be confident in myself, to let others know how much they mean to me – to be brave enough and intimate enough to make the kind of difference you made for me all of those years.

Thank you for being the kind of dad who wasn't afraid to use his hands in ways that not many fathers were willing to do. I promise your legacy will live on in me with my heart and my hands, using them both to express your eternal love for my family through me.

Never underestimate the power of a compassionate gesture. Your hands are healing. The energy that flows from your heart through your body and out of your fingertips is the love you have for the world. What a shame if you lived a full life denying your loved ones this part of you.

If you grew up never experiencing the effects of an emotional and physically affectionate mother or father, you might not know what you have been missing.

Be open to the possibility that our physical bodies are conduits of the loving energy we are all made of. We all have the ability to transfer that love and healing to others.

Why is emotional and physical affection important to the well-being of our kids?

It's all about the "power of touch." The power of touch is profoundly important to us as spiritual beings having a human experience. We need it to comfort us in difficult times because words alone don't always do justice.

We need affection to connect with each other on a deeper level. It's the glue that binds us and brings us together. The emotional and physical health benefits come by being touched in a safe and appropriate way. It is your responsibility, as the parent, to know and respect your kids, and honor them and their feelings, always checking in with them by asking them questions and expressing affection in a healthy way.

Affection brings people closer together. The welcomed touch causes the release of oxytocin, often referred to as "the cuddle chemical." It helps nurture feelings of trust and connection.

Extraordinary relationships are built upon this foundation. This foundation is important to have if you want to be influential in the life of your children.

Those who are touched safely and appropriately are more likely to cooperate, contribute, and participate in the relationship.

It's not always the grandest gesture of touch that makes the biggest impact. A quick touch on the back or holding hands can also be the difference your kids need from you to help them remember your deepest love for them.

Recently, I reached out to a good friend, Kelly Sanchez, a conscious, loving, and affectionate mother of four boys. I asked her: Why is being affectionate to your kids so important to a mother? Here is her response.

"When each of my children was born, I couldn't wait to hold them, let them sleep on my shoulder, smell them, stare at them, touch their hands and feet, the top of their ear, and feel the fuzz of that newborn body hair.

As they got older and started laughing, I couldn't wait to wiggle my face in their armpit and hear them laugh and laugh, doing it repeatedly until their belly hurt. I would tell them I love them by using my singing voice about 50,000 times a day.

When they turned two and became more independent, they liked to do things on their own, but I was always close by, ready to scoop them up and give them the kisses and the comfort they would need when they hurt themselves because they misjudged a step or two.

As they entered school, they wanted to please me so much by drawing me pictures or doing well on a test. This is when I struggled and tried to remember to cuddle up next to them, giving them hugs and kisses when they were not "producing," when they were just simply being who they are.

Middle school and high school have always been the most challenging for me. With my first son, I listened to him and said, "OK he needs space, he wants to be left alone, and he doesn't need my affection." After a few years of that monkey business and having three more boys after him, I took matters into my own hands. I decided I have to give my kids affection, no matter what they tell me.

Yes, I get it. It's a stage they go through when they want to push me away. They don't want their mom to be hanging on them, but I needed to find more creative and personalized ways to show my affection to each of my sons.

So, I did just that. For my 16-year-old, I tousle his hair when I walk by him. For my 14-year-old, I lay with him in his bed, and we watch YouTube videos on his iPad.

Occasionally, we get into a tickling match or "battle of the feet."

My 12-year-old is still open to my overly outward expressions of love, like a big bear hug in front of his classmates as I wish him a safe trip off to Yosemite. He plays it off well – rolling his eyes like, "My Mom is crazy" – but I know he loves it.

As for my 21-year-old, it's been a process of sending him text messages I think will make him laugh and inviting him to an independent film. He loves Indie films.

We hug each other often, and I always say, "I love you." He has warmed up significantly in the past two years. It gives me hope to think there is no perfect parent, but if you're willing to examine your role and reinvent yourself, the bond will never be broken.

In my humble opinion, affection is imperative at all ages and should be expressed at each stage of their life. When adolescence hits, and they push you away, you need to know they still crave your affection. I don't care what they say. It's important to find creative ways to show your affection to them.

Every child is different. It is vital, as a parent, the more you can connect with your child, the better they will feel about themselves, and the less they will go out searching and seeking negative attention or ways to connect and feel closer to others.

Hugging

"When you are hugging a child, always be the last one to let go. You never know how long they need it." - Author Unknown

It's no secret that hugging makes you healthier and happier. We have all read the statistics. Psychotherapist Virginia Satir famously said, *"We need four hugs a day for survival. We need eight hugs a day for maintenance. We need 12 hugs a day for growth."*

Some of us are not even meeting the daily minimum of 4 hugs a day.

Why is it that we can drink 8-10 glasses of water a day for our survival, yet neglect to give or receive at least the four-hug minimum, especially with people we love the most?

I can't answer that question for you, but I can reflect and share my own conclusions.

Prior to my own conscious awakening, I was not a hugger, but from what I could gather out of my own honest observations, self-reflection, and personal experience, I would have to say these factors played a part:

- I was never brought up in a family that hugged; it wasn't the norm

- I never learned how powerful hugs are, nor their benefits

- I was never encouraged to give hugs or ask for any

- As a young boy, I was too cool, or too macho, to give a hug

- I held to a limiting belief that guys don't hug other guys

- I wasn't as trusting of others as I could have been

- The fear of rejection kept me from attempting more hugs with more people

- I was too self-conscious

In my early 20s, all of that changed. I experienced a profound interpersonal breakthrough in my ability to relate to myself. I realized how guarded, protected, and safe I was with my feelings and my emotions.

The Transformational Training I attended helped me trust more, open up more, love more, express myself more and be more affectionate.

Hugging was a new challenge for me, which I happily embraced with the intention to master.

I was conditioned to protect myself for so long that it became quite the task. In fact, I had to play games with myself to create a breakthrough.

I often forced myself to say, "I love you." I would push myself to open my arms, and gesture for a hug, being 100% willing to be rejected.

After dozens of attempts, hug after hug, one "I love you" after another, the process became more effortless, more painless. To my surprise, the one thing my ego feared most – the rejection – never occurred. What an amazing breakthrough for me.

I transcended my fears because I escaped my comfort zone and challenged myself. Before I knew it, I slowly became the loving husband, father, son, and man I envisioned.

In the game I had created, I had to find some motivation to change.

I chose my kids. I chose my future grandkids to be my inspiration, to keep me courageous and valiant to stay the course and follow through with my commitment.

One of the games I played took place 30 years in the future.

I created this vision of my wife and me sitting at the dinner table of our future adult son's home. It would be Thanksgiving, and my son, his wife, and children would all be there.

In this vision or mock scenario, a day typically filled with joy and gratitude would turn out to be disappointing, an embarrassing moment filled with shame and heartbreak.

I use this imaginary vision of my adult son, who doesn't have the temperament, patience, or ability to be emotionally healthy enough to be effectively connected in his relationships.

I use the heartbreak that one might experience as a father and grandfather to help his son, and I wonder why I could not help him develop and grow into a loving father and husband.

I utilize this imaginary scenario and the depressing feeling it would give me – helpless and compassionate for my son, desperately wanting a different outcome.

I use those imaginary feelings to figure out what that lost, broken, and angry version of my son needs from me.

What he would need is this:

For his father to heal him, to build him up, to believe in him, to nurture him, to empower his greatness and become all that God intended for him to be.

Every time I think of this vision, I reach the same conclusion: My boy needs me to be the example, to be the young man I want him to be on that glorious Thanksgiving Day with his family, so he can watch me and learn.

In order to become that example, I would have to bring my walls down, allow myself to be vulnerable, to feel and be honest with those emotions.

Deep inside, I had to give up the macho act and allow myself to let him really see me. I had to let him in, let him see me hurt, see me suffer, see my fears and see me fall. However, most of all, I had to let him see me cry and see me care.

This game continued with my two daughters.

I created scenarios and visions of the men they would choose to love for a lifetime: someone emotionally healthy and powerful enough to compliment them. I knew I had to become a version of that man, who would one day show himself and ask for their hand in marriage.

I needed to become the man who was secure enough to be affectionate with them. I wanted to show them how to decide for themselves that they deserve to be loved, appreciated, and adored for who they are and the beauty they bring to the relationship.

As a part of my practice, I focused on giving my wife, kids, mother, father, sisters, nieces, and nephews as many hugs as possible, whenever possible.

Since I needed much practice, I offered hugs to my friends, aunts, uncles, cousins, neighbors, clients, and occasionally, random strangers, until I became really good at it.

Listed below are a few takeaways from my journey of hugs:

- The percentage of rejection for a hug was approximately 2%

- By the time one of my hugs was turned down, it was no longer perceived as a rejection

- People are dying for a hug but would rather take a bullet than being the first to offer it

- Every time you hug someone, you remind them how much they love it and need it

- The more you hug people, the easier it gets

- Hugs are free but require a deposit: courage

- Hugs are opportunities to know: We exist, we are here, and we matter

- There is healing energy within a hug when the intention is pure and loving

- Hugging has physical, emotional, and spiritual benefits

- **Below are a few of my affirmations:**

- It only takes one person to start a hug

- If I want people to hug me more, I have to teach it

- Hugs are contagious

- The most immediate impact I can make with my family is to offer a hug

- Hugs can heal, improve, and restore my relationship with my teenager

- One great hug is more effective than 100 apologies

- To make an "I love you" thorough and complete, seal it with a hug

- If I am in an area where a lot of people are congregated and my arms are open wide, someone with a huge heart will hug me without me saying a word

- My kids need and want more hugs from me, but the fear of rejection stops them

Suggestions on how to manifest affection:

- Create a moment of eye contact and an endearing smile

- Give someone a high five

- Give a pat or rub on the head as a gesture of endearment

- Offer a playful nudge

- Initiate a gentle caress or stroking of the face or hair

- Grant someone a kiss on the head or forehead

- Put your hand on the shoulder or back of someone to let them know you care

- Playfully tickle someone briefly

- Create a special handshake as a way to connect

- Walk up and give someone a quick 5 second back rub or neck massage

- Deliver a wink to someone to symbolize you acknowledge them

- Snuggle on the couch to share a moment

- Donate your hand gently with someone you care about

If your kids are not used to you being affectionate, and you want to introduce it into the relationship, start slow, so you don't overwhelm them. Maybe you can introduce a high five or a hand on the shoulder and then observe their reaction.

If, and when, your child has displayed a positive response to your affection, invite them to sit on your lap or sit close to you on the couch.

One of my favorite ways to show affection with my kids is to wrap my arms around them and watch them try to squirm out as I gently tickle them either with my hands or with my chin. It's the young adult version of wrestling on the floor.

My kids act as if they don't like it, but as we both laugh and become playful, the energy is loving and light-hearted. When I let them go, I feel the bond and the connection we created. Every time we do this ritual, it appears that it was well needed for both of us and long overdue. Even if they say, "Stop," or try and push you away, it's just their way of dealing with the awkwardness and newness of it.

This kind of affectionate and playful relationship is like building blocks: Each time you create a new moment, you stack new levels and the relationship blossoms. If you stay the course, you will have a pillar and a strong foundation.

In between an affectionate, playful moment, my kids are more open with me and will reach out to me more.

It's a small and beautiful window, which opens for a brief moment, offering magical opportunities to share with each other. It slowly fades away as soon as we crawl back to our busy lives.

I hope that, in this chapter, I was able to introduce possibilities, to see how much more your kids may need from you. Assure them they are, and always will be, loved by you and that you care deeply for them.

I know you love your children with all of your heart. I want your kids to be able to experience and feel that love you have for them, so in those moments they are sad, afraid, lost, or confused, they remember that you are always there for them.

I want them to realize for themselves, through your affection, that they can turn to you for advice and/or guidance anytime.

More importantly, I want you to feel a deeper sense of love, connection, and joy from your kids. You deserve to have amazing relationships with your children, filled with fun, excitement, and joy as you guide them into adolescence and adulthood, empowering them to make better decisions.

One of the questions I want to make sure I have answered is: "Who do I need to be to change?" The answer is: courageous, vulnerable, and honest, as you express your love to your child, constantly reminding them that you love and care for them.

Change is not a one-time deal. To change, you must reinvent yourself daily, constantly challenging yourself out of your comfort zone, willing to risk your pride, fears, and ego.

Suggested Homework/Activities:

- Make a new conscious commitment to re-engage with your teenager, introduce a new affectionate Mom or Dad willing to re-connect via eye contact, facial expressions, and touch.

- Find three opportunities to authentically high-five your kids, validating something special they did, something they shared, or something you noticed.

- Select one night a week to go into your son/daughter's room and show some interest. Seize the moment to hang out longer if they respond positively. Be playful and affectionate.

- Invite your son/daughter to sit close to you, and hold their hand as you acknowledge something they did.

- The next time you feel overwhelmed or frustrated, call your son or daughter into the room, ask them if they are willing to help you, and when they say yes, ask them for a hug.

- Ask your child to go for a short walk to catch up and at some point, either hold their hand or put your arm around them.

DISTINCTION TWELVE
GRATITUDE

For as long as I have been a Life Coach, I have had the honor and privilege to coach parents. Helping them create successful relationships with their children has always blessed me with internal rewards and fulfillment that never gets old.

The satisfaction and joy that comes along with being of service are priceless. I am humbly grateful for such an opportunity.

During my years of supporting parents, I have observed some common trends.

I hope that by sharing some observations and insight, you will gain value and make the appropriate course corrections to create the desired results while experiencing the joy of manifesting the kind of relationships you yearn.

One of the key elements among the frustrated parents I have counseled is uncertainty: needing a better understanding of one important distinction they seem to either lack clarity in or overlook.

However, when parents gain clarity on one important distinction, applying this fundamental principle in their relationships, it almost always leads them to become a more effective parent. They experience deeper connections with their family, and it enriches their lives tremendously.

The distinction is Gratitude.

When I decided to tackle the daunting task of adding this magical ingredient to my book, I turned to one of the best-seasoned Transformational Trainers in the business: a loving, compassionate and spiritual leader, Charlene Afremow.

I called upon Charlene and asked her to help me with this chapter. Charlene and I spent a good amount of time consulting on how to best serve you, how to help you better understand the power of gratitude, and how to use it effectively to enhance your relationships, including the ones with your children.

This entire chapter is written through the wisdom, insight, and clarity of Charlene's contribution.

I hope you receive tremendous value from this chapter, and I hope gratitude becomes a part of your daily life, bringing you joy, love, and peace.

Gratitude is a universal principle. It's been here long before us. We were born in a world that already had its own language, as well as some fundamental principles that were bestowed upon us, with the intention to use them for a greater good, to help guide us to live happily and harmoniously.

As a parent, why is it important for me to be grateful?

Success builds upon itself. To achieve success in anything, there must be some small, consistent victories that build upon each other, creating a momentum that gains strength. Success becomes a powerful energy that steam rolls you right through the finish line, creating your desired result.

Gratitude is the glue holding all your efforts together, the structure or platform you need to build upon until you reach a place where you start to recognize victory in your relationships.

As a secondary component, consistent gratitude intently and consciously fine-tunes your parental temperament or context, allowing a healthy relationship to grow and flourish.

In other words, it will help you become the safe, open, trusting, calm, positive, and reassuring parent your children need.

From their perspective, you get to show up to them as an open invitation, inviting them to engage with you, so they feel heard, appreciated, and respected.

Please remember, the way your kids see you is not the way you view yourself.

You see yourself as a loving, patient, and understanding parent; however, from their perspective, you only show up like that momentarily.

So, let's get started on exploring the distinction of gratitude. I invite you to read this chapter not from a place of validating, agreeing, or disagreeing with this information, but from an openness to learning extraordinary gratitude.

Simply put, gratitude is the awareness of all of your blessings.

"You don't have to experience being grateful or feel it," Charlene says. "It's not necessarily a feeling; you just get to *be* grateful. If you are trying to have a feeling or an experience of gratitude, you won't feel it. Gratitude may show up as a feeling, but it's not a feeling; it's a clearing – a space of appreciation and being thankful."

When she says, "Just *be* grateful," I think of all the moments when I can't see anything to be grateful for.

However, I know in the deepest part of my soul, when I am able to look through my "Soul Eyes," I see all my blessings.

When I'm not looking through my "Soul Eyes," it appears that my blessings are transparent, and I look right past them.

The trick is to train yourself to look through your "Soul Eyes," and do it more often, to see more of the blessings you have in your life. Focus on these blessings to create a new habit, a new behavior, or a new way of living.

Gratitude is a way of life.

One of the world's leading scientific experts on gratitude, Robert Emmons, writes, "Gratitude is an affirmation of goodness. We affirm there are good things in the world: gifts and benefits that we receive."

This is true if you have developed a healthy perspective to see the goodness. The challenge comes into play for those who haven't yet developed a healthy perspective.

Many of my clients have shared with me, that through their preconceived notions of the past, they are challenged in their ability to see all the good in life. Some of them honestly say it doesn't come so easily or natural for them.

Some share that the kind of childhood they had, or the kind of trauma they have experienced, has altered their perspective on life to the point that they always look for and focus on the negatives in their lives.

This kind of honest observation and acknowledgment has led most of them to discover that mindset is unhealthy and sabotages the kind of parent they wish to be.

Because we are creative beings, what we focus on, we create more of.

If you focus on the negative perspectives in your life, you keep creating more results that are negative.

If you train yourself to focus on the positive perspectives and the goodness or blessings you have in your life, you will keep creating more of those experiences.

The trick is to learn how to convert all that you see as negatives to be positives in your life. This may take some time, but with practice and intention, I assure you it's possible. It is happening, and it's a more powerful way to parent your kids and live your life.

There are different levels of gratitude. In this chapter, we will mainly focus on the first level.

The first level of gratitude is in the awareness and the practice. One would first need to be aware of the things you are grateful for, and then practice.

Think of it more like a choice, something you consciously choose to appreciate.

At first, gratitude is a decision you make to be thankful for this or that; eventually, it's a decision to be thankful for whatever you choose, ultimately leading you to be thankful for all of it: everything and everyone.

If the thought of being thankful for everything seems overwhelming, or too big to wrap your mind around, then start your practice off proportionate to what you can handle.

Find one to three things a day that you can be grateful for, gradually working your way up to being grateful for 100 things a day. Eventually, you learn how to be grateful for all of it.

Remember, it's a process – a course of awareness and practice. It may not happen overnight, but with rigorous repetition, you will soon become eternally grateful.

For me, gratitude is a perspective shift. It's a choice to alter your point of view about something that can easily be identified as a negative and transition into identifying it as a positive.

This perspective shift reminds me of a poem I read a few years back. It was a collection of suggestions to help remind me I have options, and I can choose the empowering perspective of each scenario, rather than the disempowering ones.

Most people in our society are conditioned through the years to always look at life from one perspective: "We always have to be winning." When life doesn't look like we're winning, we choose to let that process affect us negatively.

If you develop a growth mindset, you understand that life is designed to be challenging. It's meant to have ups and downs, peaks and valleys, but even in moments of challenge, there are still blessings being bestowed upon us.

Be Thankful ~Author Unknown

Be thankful that you don't already have everything you
desire.

If you did, what would there be to look forward to?

Be thankful when you don't know something,

For it gives you the opportunity to learn.

Be thankful for the difficult times.

During those times, you grow.

Be thankful for your limitations,

Because they give you opportunities for improvement.

Be thankful for each new challenge,

Because it will build your strength and character.

Be thankful for your mistakes.

They will teach you valuable lessons.

Be thankful when you're tired and weary,

Because it means you've made a difference.

It's easy to be thankful for the good things.

A life of rich fulfillment comes to those who

Are also thankful for the setbacks.

Gratitude can turn a negative into a positive.

Find a way to be thankful for your troubles,

And they can become your blessings.

Now let's take a moment and address a possibility that keeps most parents from reaching a higher level of gratitude in their parenting.

Most parents try to "fix" their kids, as though something is wrong with them.

"We are all perfect, whole, and complete," Charlene says. "There is nothing to fix. The practice of gratitude starts with the process of disappearing or clearing what is in the way of being whole, perfect and complete for yourself and another."

Parenting Scenario:

"There is something wrong with my daughter. She doesn't open up to me and share anymore. She has become secluded from the family, pushing us away."

Charlene's Response:

Unconsciously, we deny our kids the freedom to be who they are, but authentic and lasting gratitude can help us change that.

Gratitude is not being thankful for people and/or situations who are good or bad; it's not being grateful for how someone should or shouldn't be. Gratitude is about being thankful for people and situations the way they already are or aren't.

When you come from being grateful – thankful that you have a daughter, and thankful that she is the way she is – you're not resisting her. You're not trying to change her. You're just being grateful for whatever she is dealing with at this stage of her life.

If you approach interactions with her from a state of gratitude, you will quickly see there is nothing wrong with her — she is perfect the way she is. Your daughter is the way she is, and she is the way she is not.

So, what does it take from you, as the parent, to be willing to give up those preconceived beliefs about who your children are?

Ridding yourself of the mindset that you have to fix your children takes conscious practice.

In each interaction with your child, give up the idea of who you think she should be, as well as who you think you should be with her, so you can both be freed up to just be with each other.

If you can do that for your children, you become the safe space for your daughter to be the way she is: perfect.

Love is giving people the space to be authentic, and the moment we stop resisting or attempting to change another person's authenticity, our love for them becomes real.

I encourage you to consider a small possibility; In your parenting, you may operate from a psychological resistance to your kids, as they choose who they want to be along their personal journey in life.

Parents may ask their children: Why are you doing it like this? Why aren't you doing it like that? I can't believe that you did that.

Here's one of the best pieces of advice Charlene gave me personally: "You have to first learn how to relate to what they are going through. Start off by making them feel ok, and then you can move into dealing with the issue. You have to create the space of gratitude, for the fact that you even have a child, then you can begin to start supporting them more effectively. Being in resistance to what is and being unable to relate to that, will sabotage your efforts."

I ask you this important question: Are you willing to learn to be in a non-judgmental space for your kids, and to show up — no matter how they decide — without you resisting their choice?

This frees you up, to be the kind of parent they need, creating an opening for them to let you in, allowing you to advise them on how to navigate their challenges?

This is the kind of freedom sought by most parents. This is the kind of freedom most teenagers want from their parents in order to have a healthy and powerful relationship.

"I have an arthritic thumb," Charlene said. *"So, I just choose to Be grateful for my thumb. I don't make it bad or wrong. I don't say it should be this way or that way; it's just the way it is. It's just an 80-year old thumb. I'm grateful that I have a thumb, and that I am alive."*

First, things are the way they are, and then we make up stories about them being all kinds of other things. We create our own reality once we give it meaning.

For example, my son comes home late without calling to let me know he is ok. First, before anything, I know he just came home late. Everything after that; I bring into my reality and give meaning.

I am the one who decides he was wrong for not calling me I decided he was irresponsible and he doesn't respect me enough to give me a courtesy call, instead of first being grateful that he is home, safe, and alive.

From that space called gratitude, I can now see my son is not his choices or his behaviors. I can remember that he is perfect, whole, and complete. I'm grateful for the scenario because, if I'm open to it, it gives me valuable feedback: There is more that I need to teach him about responsibility, respect, and communication.

From a space of being responsible for teaching my son how to be a self-directed leader, I can clearly see that I have not taught him how to effectively communicate with me, to relieve some of my own fears about his lateness. By making multiple shifts in perspective, I have created many opportunities to show up to my kids in an inspiring and empowering way. These shifts have freed me up, to be honest with him, to be proactive while seeking powerful solutions. I wasn't reactive, frustrated, or judgmental, which may have caused resistance and an argument.

Earlier, we paused to take a moment and address a possibility that keeps most parents from reaching a higher level of gratitude in their parenting: the "trying to fix my kids" mindset.

I would like to add a letter from a teenager to her parents. This is a very courageous and inspiring letter, offering her parents some insight as to what she specifically needs from them to have a better relationship.

I wish more teens would give themselves permission to look deep into their own heart, to find the right words to say to their parents, requesting in a powerful way what they need most.

I wish that more parents like you, who are open minded, were willing to create a safe and loving space for their kids to share, give the necessary feedback, and make requests from their parents to ask for what they need.

I hope you find value while reading it.

What I Need From You

Dear Mom & Dad,

I am writing this letter to you with an open heart that is filled with hope and promise. I wish that I could talk to you directly, but I don't yet have the courage and the confidence to speak to you like this.

There are so many things I need from you, as my parents, to help raise me in a healthy way.

What I need most from you is to not try to fix everything that you see wrong with me, or that is going wrong in my life. I need you to stand by me, ready to assist me when I ask for it. More importantly, I need you to love me and believe in my ability to handle the challenges I face in my own life.

I really need you to see that I am greater than my circumstances, and I need you to remind me by constantly speaking into my greatness, rather than constantly pointing out my faults and flaws.

When you are consistently focused on what I am not doing right, or what I should be doing, it really confuses me. It obstructs my ability to believe in myself and develop a stronger self-esteem.

I know that you love me and that you want the best for me, but you cannot force me to have a great life — the way that you've imagined it.

The best thing you can do for me is not parent me with fear, reacting to all the miscalculated choices I've made. Instead, be there for me mentally, emotionally, and spiritually, and pick me up when I've fallen.

What I need most from you is to be compassionate when I am struggling and trying to figure out how to deal with the obstacles in my life.

What I need from you is to let me struggle. I need you to see that struggling is a good thing, a healthy process for me, which will teach me resilience, tenacity, and perseverance. Please don't jump in and taint that process for me, by interfering.

What I need from you is to not take it personally when I don't listen. It's not about you. It's just the way I deal with whatever is going on — it's the only way I know how. Please trust that, if you get out of the way and let this process unfold organically, I will learn the lessons I need to learn from life.

What I need most from you are plenty of hugs, plenty of smiles. Tell me often: "Atta girl," "I believe in you," and "I am proud of you."

I need you to ask me more open-ended questions, causing me to think, self-reflect, and come to my own conclusions, discovering my own answers.

What I need from both of you is to know the difference between who I am and the choices that I make or that I don't make.

Please keep seeing me in all of my magnificence, as a possibility for greatness, never losing sight of your vision of me reaching my full potential.

Mom, Dad, what I need most of you is to be grateful that we have each other to learn from, me from you, and you from me.

Let's be grateful together that we have this relationship, as an opportunity to know ourselves as a loving, caring, and compassionate family.

I am grateful for you, Mom and Dad because you are open to hearing me in this letter as though I was standing right in front of you: the courageous and confident woman I aspire to be someday soon.

Love always, Sarah

"The sun is always shining," Charlene says. "There are clouds over the sun, and what you are doing is just clearing out the clouds. You don't need to fix them, just get out of the way because they have lost themselves.

Parents need to be responsible and accountable for laying down some ground rules. As a parent, you cannot come from a place of trying to be liked by your child because you won't be able to do your job.

A lot of parents try to make their children happy instead of getting their job done, which is being committed to teaching our children to be responsible human beings."

"There are three levels of gratitude," Charlene says. "Level one starts by becoming aware of the blessings you have when you wake up in the morning. For example, your hands, your eyes, they are bright and shiny, etc."

"We start offering gratitude all day long for everything," she said. "It starts to make gratitude real for us when we practice rigorously, saying it out loud to ourselves a thousand times a day, like affirmations.

We also can affirm our gratitude if we write it down, in a gratitude book.

The second level of gratitude begins with practicing how to see the universal arrangement in your whole life. Charlene suggests; to think of it as a training of yourself – learning who we really are and who another is, and seeing it as a creative possibility.

Charlene calls the third level of gratitude: I am grateful; let me show you.

The third level of gratitude is shown through actions of appreciating someone; it is in the giving. Coming from a place of, "Let me show you," is reciprocal giving.

Saying it — and not doing it — is like wrapping a gift and not giving it away.

We really have to do something to demonstrate our gratitude otherwise it is not complete and fulfilling.

I sincerely hope you practice and become masterful at being more grateful in your life. I hope that, out of your own gratitude, you are able to tap into the parenting wisdom that is already within you.

I hope, through your journey, you can learn how to be grateful for things in advance, calling forth all of your blessings.

I hope, through your lifestyle of gratitude, you realize life's greater lessons: There is a designed plan for you and your family; you are capable of training yourselves to live spiritually and powerfully. Ultimately, you can see and know your life is a blessing.

Gratitude comes from nothing: NO-THING. That means you create it, you are the author, and you manifest it.

"As I personally look back at my life, I see how much of my life has changed by learning this simple universal principle: overwhelming gratitude at a deep, profound core — the source of love and aliveness." – Charlene

<hr>

Here are a few suggestions on how to create and practice the art of gratitude:

Start a gratitude journal. Keep it next to your bed on your nightstand and every night write down all the things for which you are grateful.

If you are a techie, download a gratitude journal app for your phone or your computer and set reminders periodically throughout your day to force you to stop and reflect.

If you are spiritual, learn some prayers of gratitude. In many spiritual traditions, being intentionally grateful is considered the most powerful form of prayer.

Make a conscious commitment to practice gratitude, with yourself, or practice it with others by supporting each other in your commitments.

Use visuals, like a gratitude board, to remind yourself of all the things you are grateful for. For example, buy a foam board and display a collection of pictures, images, or symbols that make you grateful.

Find things in your home that you don't use anymore, and give them away to others who could find a use for them. Use the practice of gift giving to symbolize your gratitude for having that item and the blessings it brought you at one point.

Write down all the things, events, and people in your life you perceive to be negative. Create a list, and then practice shifting your perspective to see if you can find a new empowering meaning for those things.

Make a commitment to give up complaining, criticizing, or gossiping for two weeks, and if you slip, replace it with a new perspective: You've found the learning lesson or the blessing in the scenario.

CLOSING

I want to congratulate you on your commitment and dedication to learning how to become a more conscious parent.

Reading and storing the information doesn't create change or manifest new results in one's life.

Your next step into conscious parenting is to practice what you've learned.

When you parlay the new-found insight, you've discovered and implement it into your daily life with your family, you will create the results you are looking for; making a big impact.

You have learned the principles of authenticity, awareness, patience, commitment, responsibility, appreciation, gratitude, vulnerability and the values of each.

Even though you may have learned some great new insight from this book, you can only expand and grow when you use these principles and their value.

It is my intention to inspire you to make the necessary growth changes within yourself that create effective and meaningful relationships with your children.

I want you to know how truly blessed your kids are to have you as their mom or dad. You kept reading to this point and it says a lot about dedication and love for your kids.

Your relentless pursuit into figuring out how to give them your all is a legacy I am proud and honored to be a part of. I think of you as a committed warrior and heartfelt leader for your family.

Thank you for sharing your time with me, and for trusting me with your heart.

I am honored to be a part of your tribe - Sawubona.

ABOUT THE AUTHOR

Alex Urbina is a veteran Teen and Parent Strategy Coach, Life Advisor, and Transformational Teen and Parent Trainer. With over two decades of experience in the personal development industry, combined with his personal experience, raising three children with his wife, Yvette, makes Alex a well-qualified Teen and Parent Expert.

During his early 20s, Alex embarked on a personal development journey. He wanted to help other people experience similar interpersonal breakthroughs, so he decided to become a Life Coach and Transformational Trainer.

Jumping in wholeheartedly to coach leadership programs for a Transformational Training Company in the greater Los Angeles area, Alex quickly developed into a powerful and passionate coach while being mentored by some of the best leadership trainers in the industry.

His passion grew intensely to make a difference in the world. When a high school teacher invited him to create a mini workshop for teenagers, it lit a fire inside him, which ultimately lead him to discover his life's purpose.

For more than 20 years, Alex has facilitated Transformational Training to help teenagers discover their personal power to live passionately, purposefully and responsibly.

In addition, Alex has facilitated training, workshops, and lectures around the U.S. and overseas to empower and inspire teens, young adults and parents.

Today, Alex continues to coach and mentor teens, parents, educators, and business owners in training rooms and in one-on-one sessions. Alex is a Radio Personality and co-hosts his own show called "The Inspirational Parent" along with his 22-year-old daughter, Jazmine, on KHTS Radio in Santa Clarita, California.

www.theinspirationalparent.com

www.alexurbina.com

www.twitter.com/alexreyurbina

www.facebook.com/themagicalingredients